Copyright © 2020 Sandie Johnson

All rights reserved.

This work reflects the author's present recollection of her experiences over a period of years. Certain names, locations, and identifying characteristics have been changed to protect the identity of the acquaintances.

All rights reserved, including the right to reproduce this book or portions thereof in any form whatsoever.

For information about special discounts for bulk purchases, please contact:

info.MsSandiejae@gmail.com

Author is available to do live events as well as virtual with a 30-day request email sent to the above address.

All vocabulary was taken by utilizing Websters Dictionary

ISBN: 978-0-578-67260-1

Thank you and Acknowledgements

First and foremost, I want to thank my creator for blessing me with the ability to express myself on paper. I remember as a kid I never liked to write, and when I became a teenage girl, it was as if that is all I wanted to do! But that push from my ancestors allowed me to "sit down somewhere" and take the time and energy to create pictures with words. For this I am forever grateful.

To Marques J. (My spouse) and my handsome young boys Isaiah, Elijah, and Noah. I thank you for your willingness to be patient with me and love me and care for me even when you didn't feel up to it. You guys all reside at the center space in my heart and I hope that when I allow you to read this book, you all know that I thought of how this could impact not only the lives of the students I mentor, but also my immediate family! You all are my true blessings and not a day goes by I don't think of how to be great to be an amazing representation of me for you!

Shout out to my brothers and sisters (Too many to name) those that I am close with and those I am not who have helped to shape and mold my way of thinking and the ability to have an impact on my life good or bad.

Huge thank you to all my mentors, confidants, and advisors for the opportunity to work under you all and learn and be developed in my adult life. Those that pushed me to recreate this book and tell the whole truth and nothing but the truth about my experiences. You all are Amazingly created, and I wish you all the Love and Success in your future endeavors with your businesses.

Last but most certainly not least I want to give a special shot out to my "Crazy mama" and my "absent father." I love and respect you both and at times I wondered if I would make the two of you proud, although I tried very hard to be and do all that was asked of me (My mom would say otherwise). But I pushed the envelope. And I took chances, and I rebelled because I got away with it a lot of the time. My mother was a single parent for the most part and she did better than she even thought she could! I thank my father for trying from afar. On the other side of the country, the relationship we established was very much appreciated and I thank you, sir, for trying although unknowing in how to be a present father.

CONTENTS

Chapter 1
Those hands don't belong there

Chapter 2
A smack on the butt

Chapter 3
Friend of the family or nah?

Chapter 4
Kids traveling alone? Where they do that at!?

Chapter 5
Your tongue doesn't belong there!

Chapter 6
I told him to stop!

Chapter 7
Just keep on driving playa

Chapter 8
Bully beatdown

Chapter 9
An unforgettable trip

Chapter 10
The Chat line part 1

Chapter 11
The chat line unfortunate part 2

Chapter 12
Women can be something else!

Chapter 13
The laundry mat

Chapter 14
My brother's friend

Chapter 15
No means N to the O!

Chapter 16
"My Stepdaddy ain't no good"

Chapter 17
All boy party

Chapter 18
Just me and my boyfriend

Chapter 19
Oh, my virginity

Chapter 20
Sweet and Sexy Sixteen

Chapter 21
Sixteen and Sassy

Chapter 22
My best friends' drunken brother

Chapter 23
My homegirls man

Chapter 24
"Your too old playa"

Chapter 25
Boys need protection too

Bonus Material
~Me and my mama poem
~Motivational song
~Epilogue
~How you can get involved

Motivational poets, writers, artists and inspirational quotes I wanted to share!!

"Darkness cannot drive out darkness; only light can do that. Hate cannot drive out hate; only love can do that."

"I have decided to stick with love. Hate is too great a burden to bear."

~Dr. Martin Luther King Jr.

"I've learned that people will forget what you said, people will forget what you did, but people will never forget how you made them feel."

"You may not control all the events that happen to you, but you can decide not to be reduced by them."

"We delight in the beauty of the butterfly, but rarely admit the changes it has gone through to achieve that beauty."

"You can only become truly accomplished at something you LOVE."

~Ms. Maya Angelou

"My mama always used to tell me: 'If you can't find somethin' to live for, you best find somethin' to die for"

"Don't believe everything you hear. Real eyes, Realize, Real lies"

"Happy are those who dream dreams and are ready to pay the price to make them come true."

~Tupac Amaru Shakur

"Everybody has an addiction, mine happens to be success."

"When writing the story of your life, don't let anyone else hold the pen."

"Before you give up, think of the reason you held on so long."

~Aubrey "Drake" Graham

My Mama Always Told Me…

"Turn your wounds into wisdom"

"Think like a queen. A queen is not afraid to fail. Failure is another steppingstone to greatness."

"You can have it all. Just not all at once."

"Real integrity is doing the right thing, knowing that nobody's going to know whether you did it or not."

"One of the hardest things in life to learn are which bridges to cross and which bridges to burn."

"Surround yourself only with people who are going to take you higher."

"True forgiveness is when you can say, Thank you for that experience."

"You don't become what you want, you become what you believe."

~Ms. Oprah Winfrey"

"Acceptance means that you know, regardless of what happened, that there is something bigger than you at work."

"You can accept or reject the way you are treated by other people. But until you heal the wounds of your past, you are going to bleed."

"The best students get the hardest tests."

~Ms. Iyanla Vanzant

"I believe that everything happens for a reason."

~Ms. Marilyn Monroe

Preface

To all the young girls and boys confused about who to turn to when touches go too far, just know Miss Sandie is here for you by far... ☺

Growing up we never had conversations of good versus bad touching. We never discussed who to confide in or whom the appropriate people or person was to tell "secrets" to. We never spoke of the struggles or hardships my mother endured as a child. Being the youngest of 4 children at times I felt I pulled the short stick so to speak. Sandie is the baby, so let's not tell her everything or share all the "family business" with her to warn her or make her more aware is how I used to feel.

I always felt as if my mother had less patience with me, less tolerance of foolish behavior, and held me to a higher standard because I was the youngest. I was told at about age nine (9) that I was her smartest child but don't tell my sister or brothers that! My head was pumped all the way up and I was trusted with large sums of money to "hold safe" for her, valuable jewelry, and other things I cannot mention but were valuable to her. But, being trusted but not having anyone to trust was difficult to endure for me.

I put a lot of my faith into boys and sometimes men because I felt a sense of comfort when it came to members of the opposite sex. I think growing up I saw my mom and how she managed and dealt with the men in her life and I aspired to be and do the same. Some may say stemming from a fatherless home? Many "replacements" but none who stayed around long enough to truly learn and be developed from.

I think of the experiences and situations I found myself in, and I think as a kid I did not know what to do, or who I could trust or turn to. Sharing such personal, sometimes embarrassing, secrets and experiences with others was intimidating. So, I take you on a journey of stories from my adolescence and channel my inner poet with what should have taken place with each situation. This is one of my most personal storytelling moments of my life. However, in my transparency I hope to help guide and direct our youth out of the "Lion's Den" so to speak.

My goal is to give real-life scenarios and "what to do" helpful tactics and nuggets to help our youth through those hard experiences I had to endure. Someone once told me we go through things sometimes to teach others so that they may avoid or be shielded from similar hardships. Reflections of Childhood trauma and yet there was Triumph! Some of the ages jump around a bit, but this is how I remember them. And I want to give a disclaimer that these stories are just that my stories. I am not a licensed therapist nor am I giving any advice with this body of work. If you are in a situation where you feel in harms way, threatened or anything of similarity you should contact the appropriate authorities.

Each chapter reflects the unfortunate trauma I endured in my adolescent and the situations that I would occasionally "get myself into" from time to time. Especially once I got my license and began to drive. You must understand that in my youth, I was self-sufficient, I worked at least one sometimes two jobs. But ultimately, I was unguided with little to no direction on what I wanted to do with my life. In the poems I want to inspire, reflect, and show the Triumph that I made it through! Some young girls were not so lucky, but I can look back to reflect and be vulnerable enough to share my story of what "My Mama Always Told Me" with all of you!

Chapter 1

Those hands don't belong there

It all started when I was eight (8) years old. My mother always had guests over. Our house was "jumpin" as the old folks used to say. Even if it was on a school night. But I was used to loud late-night music, a cloudy smoke filled dark living room space, and a **plethora** of family, friends and strange folks **congregating** in my house. I guess you can say entertaining guests was my mom's thing!

I was always an inquisitive, nosy little girl. So, on some of those nights, I just wanted to see what was going on. Go check out the latest dance moves or simply just enjoy the music that everyone was "vibing" to. Unbeknownst to me, someone had their eyes set noticing me noticing the party scene.

One night I was getting ready to go to sleep and I remember one of my older cousins came **meddling** around in my room. He was bumping into things trying to find his way I thought to the restroom. I pretended to be asleep because I feared if my mother knew I was still awake on a school night I was liable to get my butt whooped! I lay there like a statue and even held my breath so that my cousin could not locate me in the pitch-black room.

He slivered over to my bed and sat right next to me on the edge. I shared a room with my older brother and our bunk beds creaked and squeaked every time we applied any weight to them. I felt my blankets being peeled off my chest and away from my stomach. The smell of Newport cigarettes and alcohol reeked and wrapped around his breath.

His hand grazed over my stomach and crept down to my private parts. I lay there as still as I could as if I was playing a game of hide-and-seek avoiding being found. His chapped rugged fingers began to insert inside of my private and I could not be quiet any longer! I began to cry out trying to scream and/or try to yell for help, but he covered my mouth with his other dingy raggedy hand, and he held it there for what seemed to be an eternity to me.

The bedroom door opened, and I remember hearing a man's voice whisper "what are you doing in here?"

He quickly got up, **stumbling** over his words, explaining

he was "looking for the restroom." He scurried out of the room. I laid on my bed after that, **apprehensive** and **mortified** to even move. I turned over in my bed and cried myself to sleep. I could not understand what just happened to me. It was worse than any whooping I have ever received, and I could not understand what I did wrong to be punished this way.

The next morning, I went to shower for school and my panties were soaked with a residue of blood. I tried to express to my mother, but her response was "you just had a bad dream." I **speculated** she was still hungover from the night before. I don't believe she **comprehended** what I was trying to **reveal** to her.

At times I look back and wonder if she thought maybe possibly, I had just started my **menstrual cycle**? But I knew what **transpired** and from that point going forward I was always **hesitant** in the presence of that family member. Any time he came on the scene or showed up to a family function I made a point to flee out of his **whereabouts**!

I spoke to no one about the situation and I don't know if maybe I was **ashamed** or **embarrassed,** but I recall hearing about the same family member doing similar acts to other female family members! Young parents tend to be **reluctant** to give up or let go of the lifestyles that they had prior to having children.

My mother AKA Sexy Sandie (hence my name) was partying and entertaining guests all the way up until I was 18 years old. I don't blame my mama or despise her for the lack of hearing me out when I tried to tell her what took place; however, for the sake of keeping our children safe we must sacrifice the "turnt up" lifestyle to ensure our babies are looked after and kept safe!

As parents, we must sometimes learn the hard way. However, I know if she knew this happened to me, I would most likely still be visiting her behind bars.

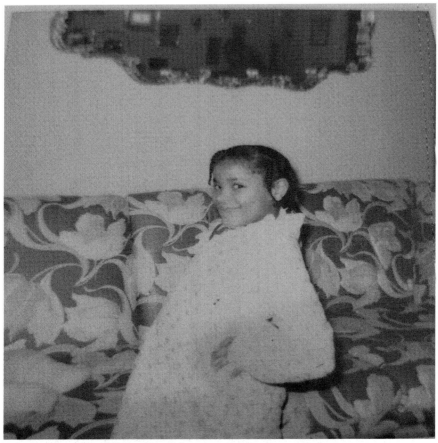

Little Sandie (Sandiego)

Poem

An old saying "**curiosity** killed the cat" to me meant if you look for trouble, you're sure to find it.
My mama would always told me trouble was easy to get into but hard to get out of.
I never imagined that curious **behavior** would cause my **innocence** to be robbed from me at such a young age,
It was like the worst act in a play or movie being acted out on the stage.
I feared getting in trouble over telling "stories"
The thought crossed my mind and man did I sit and began to worry.
No one would believe me anyway I thought,
I wrestled with how to say and what to say & what not.
You see I grew up in a family where turning a blind eye to **corrupt** behavior was almost normal to do.
My mother, and her mother, and her mother's mother as if some sick ritual set out by someone who meant my family no good.
But a voice is not just a thing to be blurred, it's a thing to be heard,
If that adult cannot compose themselves as such then they need help.
And they may not always be willing to go seek it for themselves so we must help them get help to **alleviate** them hurting someone else and causing a lifetime of **trauma** and drama.
Family or not, that man got himself hot and never got caught
If my brothers knew, I know it would have been stopped!
Listen to those little voices, don't shew them away,
What you may view as a make believe or story telling moment may just save someone's day.

Vocabulary

1. **Plethora-** "a large or excessive amount of (something)."
2. **Congregating-** "gather into a crowd or mass."
3. **Meddling-** "intrusive or unwarranted interference."
4. **Stumbling-** "tripping or losing one's balance while walking; moving with difficulty."
5. **Apprehensive-** "anxious or fearful that something bad or unpleasant will happen."
6. **Mortified-** "cause (someone) to feel embarrassed, ashamed, or humiliated."
7. **Speculated-** "form a theory or conjecture about a subject without firm evidence."
8. **Reveal-** "make (previously unknown or secret information) known to others."
9. **Comprehended-** "grasp mentally; to understand."
10. **Transpired-** "to occur; to happen."
11. **Menstrual cycle-** "the process of ovulation and menstruation in women and other female primates."
12. **Hesitant-** "tentative, unsure, or slow in acting or speaking."
13. **Ashamed-** "embarrassed or guilty because of one's actions, characteristics, or associations."
14. **Embarrassed-** "feeling or showing embarrassment."
15. **Whereabouts-** "the place where that person or thing may be found."
16. **Reluctant-** "unwilling and hesitant; disinclined."
17. **Curiosity-** "a strong desire to know or learn something."
18. **Innocence-** "lack of guile or corruption; purity."
19. **Corrupt-** "having or showing a willingness to act dishonestly in return for money or personal gain."
20. **Trauma-** "a deeply distressing or disturbing experience."

Little Sandie visiting stepfather in prison.

My Mama Always Told Me...

Chapter 2

A smack on the butt

As a child, I loved playing over my friends' houses. We would play dress up and create a whole tea party with **imaginary** friends and dolls, as well as with our favorite stuffed animals. We would do gymnastics in my friend's living room, which we enjoyed the most!

My mother would allow me to go hang out at one of my friends' houses right next door every Saturday morning. But this one **particular** day, something different happened. My friend's stepdad would always **reference** how "thick" I was as a young child (9 years old to be exact). I was a chunky girl as a child and some of my parts were larger than a child **typically** my age.

My friend's dad paid close attention to my backside, and I remember him forming his hands as a "soda bottle" reference but I had no clue what the heck he was doing. My friend and I both were doing gymnastics in her living room as we always did. We loved to do kicks and flips but mostly wanted to do headstands (attempted) and somersaults.

I began to put my hands on the floor and kick my legs in the air and suddenly, I felt a smack on my bottom. I immediately stood up and **observed** to see who this **violator** was, and to my surprise, I noticed my friend's dad looking at me staring, with his lip tucked inside his teeth. Standing directly behind me he had this sneaky demonic look on his face as if he would try and do this again if I allowed it.

I **reacted** so quickly and apologized to my friend that I had to go home. My friend cried and whined, begging me to stay but I had to go and tell someone what had happened to me. My friend was sad to see me go but I needed to run home and tell whomever I could about what took place while playing gymnastics at my friend's house next door.

When I got home, I **noticed** that my friend's mother was at my house sitting on the couch next to my mom talking (**gossiping** as usual). I thought to myself, how was I going to explain to my mom what just happened to me with the mother of my friend sitting right next to her? That would not only be weird, but it would be **awkward** to try to **explain**. This man was her husband, and I didn't want to get in any trouble.

Why I even felt like I would get in trouble for reporting what someone did to me I don't know. I did not want my friend's mom to be upset with me and not allow me to come over and play anymore. Telling my mom's friend that her husband put his hands on my bottom side would certainly stop my friend from being allowed to come over my house as well.

- What if she never let me play with her daughter again?
- How would my mom **react**?
- Would she be upset that she and my friend's mom wouldn't get to hang out anymore?

These were all the thoughts that I had going on in my mind. I **decided** not to tell anyone about my friend's stepdad. I even thought, "What if he was doing these acts to her as well?"

I decided not to go over to my friend's house and play anymore; and, she couldn't come over to my house like I could go over to hers. We didn't play with each other from that **instance** on, but I saw her at school every now and then and we played at recess together sometimes. I don't even think she realized what happened at her house that day because she was somewhat younger than I was. She probably thought that was something normal that her stepdad did. What I should have done was spoken to my mother alone **immediately** after this situation took place.

As kids we get sidetracked or fearful of what will happen if we tell about any **inappropriate** touching especially coming from an adult. We mustn't feel this way especially since we, as children, can be **vulnerable** and afraid to talk to someone. But sometimes it makes a situation worse not to say something because that person gets away with their **behavior**, which is also a crime.

The **instance** at my friend's house that her dad **committed** is not holding him responsible or **liable** for his **offense**. We must remember if someone touches us in a bad way or in any of our personal areas on our body, we have a duty and a **responsibility** to report them, so they don't have the **opportunity** to do this to someone else and hurt them.

Somebody is going to an Easter Sunday Service!

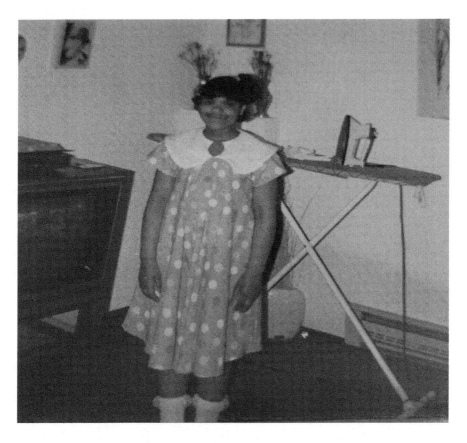

Poem

He said I was thick,
He even licked his lips.
He looked at me like I was grown,
I hated when my mama talked to his wife on the phone.
At times I felt all alone.
I don't think I did anything wrong,
Men should keep their eyes, hands and teeth to themselves,
Because it's obvious that some of them need help.
I was afraid to go off and tell,
Not knowing if the matter would end with a scream or a yell?
But I know now that he was sick,
And no man should ever tell a little girl that she's thick!
He wanted to lure me in with his tricks,
But I got ghost really quick!
I should have told my mom regardless of what I thought,
This man needed help and he should have been caught!

Vocabulary

1. **Imaginary-** "existing only in the imagination."
2. **Particular-** "used to single out an individual member of a specified group or class."
3. **Reference-** "the action of mentioning or alluding to something."
4. **Typically-** "in most cases; usually."
5. **Observed-** "notice or perceive (something) and register it as being significant."
6. **Violator-** "a person who breaks or fails to comply with a rule or formal agreement."
7. **Reacted-** "respond or behave in a particular way in response to something."
8. **Gossiping-** "casual or unconstrained conversation or reports about other people, typically involving details that are not confirmed as being true."
9. **Awkward-** "causing difficulty; hard to do or deal with."
10. **Decided-** "(of a person) having clear opinions; resolute."
11. **Instance-** "an example or single occurrence of something."
12. **Immediately-** "at once; instantly."
13. **Inappropriate-** "not suitable or proper in the circumstances."
14. **Vulnerable-** "(of a person) in need of special care, support, or protection because of age, disability, or risk of abuse or neglect."
15. **Committed- "feeling** dedication and loyalty to a cause, activity, or job; wholeheartedly dedicated."
16. **Responsibility-** "the state or fact of being accountable or to blame for something."
17. **Instance-** "an example or single occurrence of something."
18. **Behavior-** "the way in which one acts or conducts oneself, especially toward others."
19. **Opportunity-** "a set of circumstances that makes it possible to do something."
20. **Liable-** "legally responsible for causing damage or injury, so that you have to pay something or be punished."

My Mama Always Told Me...

Little Sandie going off to church
(You couldn't tell me nothing in my velvet green dress!)

Chapter 3

Friend of the family or nah?

When I was nine (9) my Uncle got released from prison. He served over 10 years at a maximum-security **institution**. My mom and other family used to throw a lot of parties as we all know, and my house was lit every Friday and Saturday sometimes even on Sunday! Smoke-filled living room, loud old school music, and dozens of people; some I knew, some I did not. This older white dude used to always be at my house during those parties.

I don't know how he knew my family, but one would call him a "family friend", I remember on this **particular** evening my Uncle was released. The old dude saw me going to the bathroom and said to me, "Hey lil mama, how old are you? Back then we would say how old we were followed by how old we would be turning or next birthday, so my response was "I'm 9 but I'm about to be 10".

I **expressed** squeezing my legs tighter together as I answered because I really had to go to the restroom and the man said to me, "You look like a grown woman girl!" He had a Southern **accent** or something I couldn't really tell, but I knew he wasn't from around here.

He asked me if I had a little boyfriend. I told him I really had to go to the bathroom, and he asked me if he could come with me? I looked at him and I yelled:
"NO THAT'S NASTY!"

I asked the man to leave me alone and I ran into the restroom slamming the door and locking it behind me. I used the toilet and once I finished, I stayed in there for what seemed to be hours. (It may have been an hour). I stuck my ear to the door to see if I could hear anyone outside the door, but the music was too loud.

The next week came and my house was **crowded** once again full of family and my mom's friends and I saw the man sitting next to one of my aunts on the couch. He **stared** at me the entire time I went to get something to drink out of the kitchen. My aunt saw me and told me to come over and meet her new boyfriend.

I thought to myself, "This man is your boyfriend?" Old dude welcomed me with his arms open to **embrace** me for what felt like nothing short of a bear hug. He then spun me around as if to look at all of my parts and picked me up and placed me on his lap. He began bouncing his leg as my aunt laughed **hysterically**.

I didn't know what was so funny about a young girl being

bounced up and down on some strange man's leg. But I asked him to stop, slid off his knee and **proceeded** to head back to my room. I closed my door and **barricaded** it good with my bed and some toy boxes that were heavy. I remember being worried he would try and come into my room and I was afraid to leave back out the rest of the night.

The next morning my mom came to wake me up for school and she couldn't get in my room and she began yelling at me asking why I have the door blocked off so she couldn't get in. I wanted to tell her why I locked myself in my room, but I was afraid I would get in trouble. Most of the time I had something to tell my mom, I always feared I would get in trouble or be **punished**, even if I hadn't done anything wrong.

I never saw the man again after that night and now looking back that man demonstrated the characteristics of a child molester. He did not belong in my momma's house and he did not belong anywhere near me at a grown folk's party.

Poem

Family friend or **foe**
You never really know
Come off one way and the whole time they will lead you to **dismay**
All shapes and sizes like an array
Those lines are every bit of gray
"Young lady you look like a grown woman" well I'm NOT!
Creepy old man tryna get what he thought!
Should have ran off and blew up his spot!
Tell my mama about the expression of his behavior
Lookin' at me like "Yeah, I think I can save her"
Pedophile most certainly he was
I said, "I'm nine sir", he looked like just because
He still would have **pursued** if I allowed him to
He wasn't around long; my aunt knew he was through!
I'm glad I knew exactly what to do...
Get from around him and stay in a child's place like my mama told us to do.
I always thought that she was being mean
But now I know she saw things I had never seen!

6th grade pictures. (I got clowned for this hairstyle for the longest!)

Little Sandie's 9th birthday turning $9 into $900!

Vocabulary

1. **Institution-** "an established law, practice, or custom"
2. **Particular-** "used to single out an individual member of a specified group or class."
3. **Accent-** "a distinctive mode of pronunciation of a language, especially one associated with a particular nation, locality, or social class"
4. **Expressed-** "convey (a thought or feeling) in words or by gestures and conduct."
5. **Crowded-** "(of a space) full of people, leaving little or no room for movement; packed."
6. **Stared-** "look fixedly or vacantly at someone or something with one's eyes wide open."
7. **Hysterically-** "with wildly uncontrolled emotion."
8. **Embrace-** "hold (someone) closely in one's arms, especially as a sign of affection."
9. **Proceeded-** "move forward, especially after reaching a certain point"
10. **Barricaded-** "block or defend with an improvised barrier"
11. **Foe-** "an enemy or opponent."
12. **Dismay-** "cause (someone) to feel consternation and distress."
13. **Pedophile-** "a person who is sexually attracted to children."
14. **Pursued-** "follow (someone or something) in order to catch or attack them"
15. **Punished-** "inflict a penalty or sanction on someone for (such an offense)"

My Mama Always Told Me...

Chapter 4

Kids traveling alone? Where they do that at!?

Have you ever **ridden** a bus to another state? Let alone cross country? Well, I have… I wasn't even afraid! I thought it would be a great **adventure** and I had no one to tell me what to do on this trip because I would be all by myself. I had no one to listen to except my radio **cassette player**.

I got all the way to Chicago and this boy got on the bus. I sat close to the front because my mom told me to be near the bus driver so he could **observe** me every now and then. When the young boy saw me, he immediately came and asked if he could sit next to me. I thought to myself, "ABSOLUTELY!" But my mama always said, "Don't be no **fast tale little girl**."

There was an empty seat in front of me, so I told him he could sit there. We began talking and we **discovered** that we were the same age, both loved cooking and were both going to visit our fathers. After talking for a whole day, we had plenty of things to talk about. We had so much in common and he enjoyed music as much as I did. Even sang me a little song which was **corny,** but he had a nice voice, **nonetheless.** We talked about where we both had come from and where we were going. Then he asked me if I had a boyfriend. (Dudes ask this as if they really care.) I told him no I did not.

I asked him if he had a girl and he **admitted** to having a "lady friend" back home. He asked me how my parents trusted me to be **traveling** alone. I **expressed** to him that I was traveling alone but I could handle myself. (This is what young girls who think they are "hard" say to not try to come off like a "punk.") We got to the next stop and a lot of people began **boarding** the bus. To **avoid** sitting next to some stranger who may be **unpleasant** I felt **confident** to invite the young guy to sit next to me.

I learned that he was 16 and not 13 by a **conversation** we had and him expressing to me a birthday party his mom threw for him (Why do guys lie about their age when the girl is younger?). At the time I was 13 and we had a **discussion** leading up to the arrival of our destination about 'freaks.'

He asked me if I knew what being a freak was. And I told him I did. He then asked me what was the freakiest thing I had ever done. I told him I didn't know. (I really felt uncomfortable answering this.) He asked me if he could kiss me. I told him I didn't even know him like that.

I was **flattered** at the fact that he was older than me but still was digging me. (Young girls feel like they're "special" when older dudes wanna spit at us, but in all **actuality**, they are just **perverts** who wanna **take advantage** because they think young chicks are **gullible** and **naïve**. A lot of the time we are!) He asked me again if he could kiss me and with a shrug of the shoulders, I told him that I didn't care. He then asked me if he could put his hand in my shirt.

I had on a pretty little yellow blouse with buttons, so it was easy to unravel and unloosen and he began to rub my breast. We were making out and feeling on each other for about 15 minutes before the bus driver yelled out, "aye girl what you at!" He couldn't see me because we were **hunched** down so far in the seat. I quickly **clenched** my shirt together and rose up to where I could see the eyes of the bus driver and he told me to make sure that I was **behaving** myself! What a life saver!

I wasn't **confident** in what would take place next. His hands were traveling farther and farther "down south" and I was fearful he would try to put his hands in my pants. The boy asked for my phone number and I gave it to him but of course, I gave him a fake number! I didn't even have a phone yet. He gave me his number and told me he was getting off on the next stop and to call him some time. I figured I would never see him again and could not wait for the bus to stop!

This journey of traveling across country alone as a child was not only **terrifying** after all but I wasn't ready to take on such a huge responsibility! I thought to myself what if the boy would have raped me or worse, **lured** me off the bus and brought harm's way to me; left me **stranded** or something? That could have been **unimaginable**.

Now I know what my mom meant about being a fast tale little girl. I guess she was right after all. Sorry mama. What my mom should have done was came with me to go see my family on the other side of the country or sent someone older and responsible with me to aid in traveling with me. I should have kept to myself and not put myself in such a dangerous situation because who knows what could have happened to me that has happened to other young girls traveling alone. ☹

I had to cut that guy out the picture he was too old for me anyway!!

Poem

"Aren't you a cute young thang," he said,
Hopping on the bus with a head full of dreads.
He was different and **charismatic** I thought,
And **flattered** at the fact he thought I was hot!
From Washington to Philadelphia that's a 3-day, 4-night trip,
Nowhere to go I could hardly try to dip!
One conversation that turns into hugging that turned into rubbing,
At the time I was **confident** I would not go further than touching.
He convinced me he was "clean" and safe
And boy did he have a cute face!
However, my behavior put me in a place of disgrace.
Hardly noticed myself even thinking of my headspace.
To convince is one thing to act is another,
I think back, I should've listened to my mother.
Don't talk to strangers she would always say,
But she never said anything about kids my age!
Some men will portray themselves as young boys too...
Especially if they sip from the "black don't crack" fountain of youth!

Vocabulary

1. **Adventure-** "an unusual and exciting, typically hazardous, experience or activity."
2. **Observe-** "notice or perceive (something) and register it as being significant."
3. **Discovered-** "find (something or someone) unexpectedly or in the course of a search."
4. **Corny-** "trite, banal, or mawkishly sentimental."
5. **Nonetheless-** "in spite of that."
6. **Admitted-** "confess to be true or to be the case, typically with reluctance."
7. **Charismatic-** "exercising a compelling charm which inspires devotion in others."
8. **Unpleasant-** "causing discomfort, unhappiness, or revulsion; disagreeable."
9. **Confident-** "feeling or showing confidence in oneself; self-assured."
10. **Conversation-** "a talk, especially an informal one, between two or more people, in which news and ideas are exchanged."
11. **Discussion-** "the action or process of talking about something in order to reach a decision or to exchange ideas."
12. **Flattered-** "lavish insincere praise and compliments upon (someone), especially to further one's own interests."
13. **Pervert-** "alter (something) from its original course, meaning, or state to a distortion or corruption of what was first intended."
14. **Take advantage-** "to benefit, gain or profit."
15. **Gullible-** "easily persuaded to believe something; credulous."
16. **Naïve-** "(of a person or action) showing a lack of experience, wisdom, or judgment."
17. **Hunched-** "raise (one's shoulders) and bend the top of one's body forward."
18. **Clenched-** "of the fingers or hand) closed into a tight ball."
19. **Confident-** "feeling or showing confidence in oneself; self-assured."
20. **Unimaginable-** "difficult or impossible to imagine or comprehend."

Chillin' at my sister's house in Trenton, NJ! I knew early not to tell her anything to refrain from having to bail her out of jail!! My sis doesn't play!!
Love you Shawnee-Pooh

Chapter 5

Your tongue doesn't belong there!

When I was a preteen, I went to visit my father and his family in Philadelphia. My father picked me up and the plan was to stay the whole summer at his house with his wife and other children. My mother and father were never in a relationship. I guess you could say it was a "Homie hook-up" type of situation? They were homies and they hooked up! But when he arrived to pick me up, he **introduced** me to his son aka my little brother Tyheem (Rest in Paradise little brother) and I was very excited to meet the rest of my family and get to know my East Coast peeps!

We drove what seemed to be almost an hour to their apartment complex, gospel music blasting out of the **airwaves** the entire car ride. My father was very much into Christianity and he lived a lifestyle where **morals** and **values** were extremely **implemented** in his household. It's kind of caught me by surprise because the stories my mother used to tell me about him were that of a street dude who could **hustle** you out of your shoes if he wanted to!

My father expressed to me the rules of his home and the **consequences** if I broke any of these rules. The number one rule was respect for adults and among a list of other rules there was to be NO R&B music or RAP music played in his house! We arrived and he welcomed me in to meet his wife and her two boys from a previous marriage. The one boy was about two (2) or three (3) years older than me.

I did not find him **attractive** at all, not to mention he was my brother through marriage, so he would have been my stepbrother. The younger brother was maybe two (2) years younger than me and although a goofy kid, he **possessed** a calm and sweet spirit. His older brother seemed mischievous and rough around the edges for the most part.

My father would take me to work with him every day. And to my surprise, he paid me the minimum, but I was thankful to have money in my pocket. I had been working and hanging out meeting my Trenton family in New Jersey for a few weeks. One day my dad came to wake me up to take me to work with him, but I was knocked out! I called him from the house phone, and he **expressed** to me "you snooze, you lose!" Because I overslept, he had to leave me at the house since his job was quite a few miles away.

At the time he delivered produce and such to local restaurants and facilities. He went over the rules again number one being to be respectful and NO R&B music or RAP music in his house! I was an R&B baby to the Max! You couldn't tell me, a young girl **infatuated** with Immature, Faith Evans, Mary J, Mariah Carey etc. not to **partake** in the love I had for music! Father or Not! (I was quite the **hard-headed** little girl my mother always told me!)

The two stepbrothers were at the house with me, and so was my little brother *Tyheem*. I flipped through the channels on the television once I got myself dressed and ate some breakfast. The channels to my **excitement** were very similar to those in Washington! As soon as I saw 106 and Park it was on and crackin'! It was one of my favorite shows back when I was home in Washington.

I watched maybe three or four videos before my evil older stepbrother threatened to **snitch** that I was breaking one of the rules in the house, which was not to play any R&B music. He tried to **blackmail** me, and his **proposition** was if I gave him a KISS, he wouldn't tell my father that I had been watching music videos! I was beyond **disgusted**! Not only was he my stepbrother he was also **unattractive** in my opinion. "I would never in a million years", I thought. I told him that was gross!
I couldn't believe he would even ask me that, we were basically related!

He tried to explain to me that we were only related by marriage, so we weren't blood. He began chasing me all over their apartment **begging** me to give him a kiss!

When I **refused,** he continued to **threaten** to tell my father and he would even pick up the phone and start to dial his number. I didn't care though! I wasn't kissing him even if it meant getting in trouble; I was willing to face my father rather than face his face!

He kept chasing me around the house and finally he caught up to me and he stuck his nasty tongue in my mouth! I probably spent a good 20 minutes after that brushing my teeth, gargling mouthwash and spitting out whatever remains of him that were left over! Talk about cooties, "YUCK!" I felt so gross and **taken advantage of**!

My stepbrother held the phone hostage because I **threatened** to call and tell my father what he had done; therefore, I couldn't even get ahold of him soon after the situation took place. My father and stepmother returned home that evening and I **immediately** went to tell them what happened. I tried to call home and tell my mom, but I couldn't get ahold of her. He not only **sexually assaulted** me, he disrespected me and tried to blackmail me, and I expressed to my father everything that took place.

My stepbrother blurted out "she was watching music videos" and my father looked at me and inquired if this was true. I looked at him as if I had not just expressed what his stepson had done to me. I was **scolded** for playing R&B music in his house and this dude lied and said I made up a story about him sticking his NASTY tongue in my mouth to avoid getting in trouble about the music!

I **demanded** to call my mother and cried on the phone for her to send for me to come home immediately. The adults who I trusted would protect me and keep me out of harm's way FAILED me at that moment in time PERIOD! I was completely disappointed, and my father made me never want to visit him again! I was taken advantage of completely and no justice was served.
I don't know if it was because my father was trying to please his wife but not tearing that boys' tale up? I lost some respect for him and couldn't imagine some music taking precedence over my child's body and a complete **violation**.

Please parents be careful of the company you leave in your children's presence even if they are OTHER children. Be careful who you decide to hang out around because their intentions are not always good. What I should have done was had a one on one conversation with my father and expressed to him how **uncomfortable** I was at his house after this situation took place. I should have urged him to send me home as soon as possible or, allowed me to stay with another family member until I could return home.

I didn't blame my father nor was I upset with him for leaving me at his house which he probably thought was safe with my other "siblings", but I was quite disappointed that when expressed to him what took place the Music Choice superseded my safety.

Poem

A no is just that, a no!
He thought I was some young pro?
I was truly ready to go!
My dad knew he let me down fa sho!
I had to avoid every **interaction** with him moving forward,
A young boy nonetheless a complete coward!
No one must have taught him to respect a girl's temple,
All because he thought I had a cute gap with a little dimple?
Family can do you wrong no doubt,
He could've found someone else to go kiss in the mouth!
I play back what I could have done different,
Maybe woke up on time and hit the working implement!?
Or took a walk once I discovered this fella had his eyes pent?
All things considered he needed a man to talk to him and express to him you respect young girls,
Don't be chasing and running to invade their world!
That mess played out in my head over and over again,
I never wanted to go visit my father since then!
It took years to go back to see my family and a couple of friends,
I was an adult and he grew up to be a young man,
I avoided being in his presence once again!
Flashbacks of torment and torture rang through my head that was on spin,
Wish I had it all over to do and call out his sin!

Vocabulary

1. **Introduced-** "bring (something, especially a product, measure, or concept) into use or operation for the first time."
2. **Airwaves-** "the radio frequencies used for broadcasting."
3. **Morals-** "a person's standards of behavior or beliefs concerning what is and is not acceptable for them to do."
4. **Values-** "the regard that something is held to deserve; the importance, worth, or usefulness of something."
5. **Hustle-** "an aggressively enterprising person; a go-getter."
6. **Consequences-** "a result or effect of an action or condition."
7. **Attractive-** "(of a thing) pleasing or appealing to the senses."
8. **Possessed-** "have as belonging to one; own."
9. **Expressed-** "convey (a thought or feeling) in words or by gestures and conduct."
10. **Infatuated-** "possessed with an intense but short-lived passion or admiration for someone."
11. **Partake-** "join in (an activity)"
12. **Hardheaded-** "practical and realistic; not sentimental."
13. **Excitement-** "a feeling of great enthusiasm and eagerness."
14. **Blackmail-** "demand money or another benefit from (someone) in return for not

revealing compromising or damaging information about them."
15. **Proposition-** "make a suggestion of sexual intercourse to (someone with whom one is not sexually involved), especially in an unsubtle or offensive way."
16. **Disgusted-** "feeling or expressing revulsion or strong disapproval."
17. **Hideous-** "extremely unpleasant."
18. **Refused-** "indicate or show that one is not willing to do something."
19. **Taken advantage of-** "treat someone unfairly for their own benefit."
20. **Sexually assaulted-** "an act in which a person intentionally sexually touches another person without that person's consent."

Boy that finger wave was Poppin!! Haha

I was always on the phone! (Just like my mama!)

Chapter 6

I told him to stop!

There once was this boy I really liked. I think he liked me too because sometimes we would sneak off and make out at school behind the **gymnasium**. He was a nice kisser and we called each other boyfriend and girlfriend. After a few weeks we would get pretty hot and heavy every chance we could get to smooch each other up!

One day he **invited** me over to his cousin's house to hang out. He didn't live very close to me, but his cousin stayed right around the corner. He told me there would be other people there so I guess you could say it was something like a house party. There were no adults that **appeared** to be home. He asked me if I wanted to go in one of the bedrooms, just the two of us.

I thought we would go somewhere to make out like we did when we were at school but this time my boyfriend asked me to take off my pants as he began to remove his own. I had never seen a boy's private part before! He began touching himself while he kissed me. I told him to stop but he kept touching and kissing anyway. I had never had sex before nor did I truly know what it was and all of my friends told me that if I did it, that mess would hurt the very first time! I was afraid to do it after hearing all that.

My boyfriend knew I was a **virgin**. He told me that I was special, and he wanted to take my **virginity**. I did not want him to touch or see my private though, so I didn't know how that was gonna happen. I knew that if I told him no or denied him, he would be mad at me. I knew that if I denied him, he would be mad at me because at school sometimes if he asked me for a kiss and I told him no, he wouldn't speak to me for a few days.

Sometimes during our little breaks, I would even hear stories about him flirting or chasing after other females. I was very **fearful** to have sex, so I told him to STOP! When he wouldn't stop or listen to me, I pushed him off me and I ran all the way home! I never wanted to be alone with him again and I told my neighbor who was a good friend from church what had taken place at my boyfriend's cousin's house!

I told my neighbor because I knew I could trust her, and I asked her not to tell my mom because I didn't want to get in trouble for not being where I should have been in the first place. She **encouraged** me to discuss this situation with my mom and let her know because she said the boy could get in trouble for what he tried to do to me.

Sometimes a boyfriend or girlfriend may try to **convince** you to do something inappropriate that you don't want to, and they try to take your fear and twist it into excitement! **Manipulation** plays a huge part in a lot of the stories I heard from my friends in how they lost their virginity and I know you must be strong and fearless enough to say stop!

My mama always told me not to go to peoples' houses without a buddy or a friend. So, I'm sorry mama I didn't listen.

Whenever going somewhere it's best to travel in groups with two or more people so that in the event something happens you have someone that can help you. If I had a friend with me, I could have yelled for help when things became uncomfortable for me. It's OK to like boys or girls but if you find yourself in a troublesome situation then you must keep yourself safe and tell them if you feel uncomfortable. If they won't listen, then you need to go and get help from someone you can trust!

Poem

My boyfriend says I'm pretty and all his friends are jealous
He says they want me for themselves and he tends to get **rebellious**
He's not even supposed to have a girlfriend his mom is very **overprotective**
I've met her a time or two and she can be very directive
Her stern demanding demeanor is where I believe he inherited these traits
I could tell right from the gate, when I told him no his eyes filled with hate
Most of the time a nice boy when I see him my heart was overjoyed
But this day he took it too far, to me he was every bit of a star
Puppy love if you will, to all my friends I wanted to spill
The tea was nice and chill
However, he crossed a line that was **unspoken**
He knew I was not some token
My heart completely broken, but my **innocence** was chosen
Respecting myself was quite the trouble
Guess that's the reason I stayed in trouble?
But on this day, I made the right choice
I chose to find my **outspoken** voice!

Vocabulary
1. **Outspoken-** "frank in stating one's opinions, especially if they are critical or controversial."
2. **Unspoken-** "not expressed in speech; tacit."
3. **Overprotective-** "having a tendency to protect someone, especially a child, excessively."
4. **Rebellious-** "showing a desire to resist authority, control, or convention."
5. **Expecting-** "regard (something) as likely to happen."
6. **Manipulation-** "the action of manipulating something in a skillful manner."
7. **Convince-** "cause (someone) to believe firmly in the truth of something."
8. **Encouraged-** "give support and advice to (someone) so that they will do or continue to do something."
9. **Fearful-** "in an anxious manner; apprehensively."
10. **Virgin-** "a person who has never had sexual intercourse."
11. **Virginity-** "the state of being naive, innocent, or inexperienced in a particular context."
12. **Appeared-** "seem; give the impression of being."
13. **Invited-** "make a polite, formal, or friendly request to (someone) to go somewhere or to do something."
14. **Gymnasium-** "a room or building equipped for gymnastics, games, and other physical exercise."
15. **Innocence-** "lack of guile or corruption; purity."

My Mama Always Told Me…

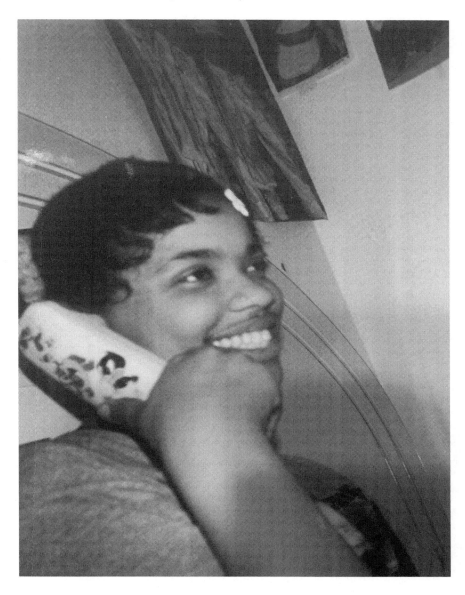

My Mama Always told me "Sandie,
GET OFF THE PHONE!" 😊
Middle school was a pivotal time in my life.

My Mama Always Told Me…

Chapter 7

Just keep on driving playa

In 10th grade I remember how I couldn't wait to get a car! I remember I would **imagine** myself driving my mom's car every day after school. I recall on my way home this guy used to pull up beside me in his red Chevy Impala and try to get me to hop in the car with him. Every week he would find me walking down the street, even if I went a different way. It was like he was **stalking** me or something!

I can hear his brakes screech as he **approached** me and with his gold teeth placed where his fangs would be, he would ask "aye pretty girl do you need a ride?" Weeks went by, an old no-name continued to harass me! One day we went hard in PE and honestly, I was just too tired to walk home, and I guess you could say on that day I called myself looking for old dude to pull up.

I got halfway to my home and there came the screeching

of these worn out breaks.

"Aye pretty lady," he yells out from the passenger side window, "you need a ride?

This time after practically two (2) weeks of flat out stalking me on my way home, I told the fella "yeah I'll take a ride!" I was tired yawl. What can I say?! I agreed purely due to **exhaustion,** but "it wasn't like I wasn't already home or close to home" I thought!

My mama always told me "Don't talk to strangers!" We watched that unsolved mysteries show for years and I remember my mom explaining to me what happens to kids who talk to strangers! But my fearless mentality felt like I could handle myself just fine.

I really didn't want him to know where I lived, let alone let my mom's see me pulling up to the house with some grown man and his bright red Impala! I would get my butt tore up for sure! I asked old boy what his name was, and he told me it was PRIORITY... "What kind of name is that?" I asked. He told me it was a nickname because all his ladies knew that when he called, they better make it a PRIORITY to respond! So, I asked him his real name and he quietly said Roland.

"You don't like your real name?" I asked. Then he quickly changed the subject and asked me my name. Back then my **alias** was Sasha! Not to be confused with Ms. Sasha Fierce (Beyoncé). My mom told me she wanted to name me that before she named me Sandie.

So, PRIORITY asked if he could take me on a date to dinner and a movie. Shoot yawl I was a chubby little girl and I loved to eat! So, my fast tale self, as my mama would say, agreed and I told him to meet me at the mall Saturday! That way I could tell my mom I was hanging out with one of my friends from school. He agreed, and I hopped out of his car quickly and **sprinted** behind the house he dropped me off at a couple doors down.

Saturday came and I posted up in front of the Mall waiting on PRIORITY to pull up. Screech, screech.... I knew that **distinct** sound anywhere. I wore a long black maxi dress and cleavage-revealing blouse. Trying to be grown as the old folks would say, and although I had no clue how to apply makeup, I managed to brush on some eye shadow over my eyelids and yawl know my lip gloss was poppin'!

I hopped in the car making sure to be seen first of course. This is my first "date" and it was with a man at least two (2) times my senior. He smelled good but most of the car reeked of marijuana sticks! He told me I looked beautiful and I said, "Thank you, you don't look too bad yourself." He chuckled. **Validation** from men was always a necessity to me.

I know they call it **self-esteem**, but if a dude wasn't checking for me, I knew I had to step my game up! He drove to this little raggedy steakhouse in Tacoma. He opens my door for me and everything y'all. Told me to order whatever I wanted, and you know I did! He sat close to me and kept trying to put his hand on my leg rubbing and kissing on my neck and what not. I **nudged** his hand over and over until finally the food came out. "Thank God," I thought!

And yawl know how those Japanese steakhouses get to putting on a good show! Flipping and talking mess, throwing chicken and shrimp all over the place "Hoo-ha-heyyyyyy." We ate most of our food and PRIORITY asked if I was ready to go? I asked if we were going to the movies? His response... "Nah lil' mama I had something better in mind?"

I looked at him as if I didn't know what he was talking about. He **flumped** in on the driver side of the seat and waited for me to open my own door this time. I thought to myself "how rude!" but I got in the car and he continued to put his hand on my leg, creeping up more and more towards my inner thigh. I asked if he could take me home.

He expressed, "why lil mama? Ain't you having a good time? I thought we were having a good time?"

I don't know why he thought that? We didn't talk at the restaurant at all. He was too busy rubbing all over me and stuffing his face with food! He never even asked me how old I was and seeing me at the high school all the time I know he had to know I was a student!

PRIORITY took a **detour** on the way to my house and I asked where we were going? He **expressed** to me "we 'bout to slide to my crib!"

His house!?? I thought! Ohhhh heck no!!! I told him I

just wanted to go home, and he said he had a surprise for me at his house. "Negro I don't want nothing you got at your spot!" I thought. In my mind I said to myself he was too big to fight if need be so as soon as he stopped at the next red light I shoved the door open and jumped out the car leaving the door open and ran as fast as my fat little legs could! We were about a mile away from my house, but I swear I ran all the way there it seemed.

I got home and was quickly **approached** by my mother talking about "where have you been?"

"I just came from one of my friends' house," I said. My mama said, Which one? And why are you breathing so hard?" So, I made up a name in case one of them heffas called me while I was out! I thought it was about to start raining I explained and that was normal in Tacoma!! She told me to go to bed! I thanked God nothing bad happened to me that night, and from then on, I asked my mom to pick me up from school or I convinced one of the homies to walk with me and I never saw PRIORITY again!

Poem

You a grown behind man, I don't understand
What you see in a young girl, aside from the thought of luring her in!
As if dinner and a movie could convince me
To be on defense see, could you please take and do away with what you thought could be?
I'm not that kind of girl you see, he approached so **cowardly**,
Flossin and flexin like he sought out to be with me
Predatory stalking his prey, no matter the direction I took any day
He saw the **hesitation** in my no
And decided I'll wear her down as time passes to go
My mama would always say, "You ain't grown"
At least that's what she would say when she wanted me off the phone!
Stay young as long as you can, especially when it comes to dealing with a grown man!
Don't get caught up or stuck, I **escaped** what could have left me out of luck!

Vocabulary

1. **Escaped** "having broken free from confinement or control."
2. **Hesitation**- "the action of pausing or hesitating before saying or doing something."
3. **Predatory**- "seeking to exploit or oppress others."
4. **Cowardly**- "in a way which shows a lack of courage."
5. **Approached**- "come near or nearer to (someone or something) in distance or time."
6. **Detour**- "long or roundabout route that is taken to avoid something or to visit somewhere along the way."
7. **Flumped**- "fall or sit down heavily."
8. **Nudged**- " prod (someone) gently, typically with one's elbow, in order to draw their attention to something."
9. **Validation**- "the action of making or declaring something legally or officially acceptable."
10. **Self-esteem**- "confidence in one's own worth or abilities; self-respect."
11. **Distinct**- "recognizably different in nature from something else of a similar type."
12. **Sprinted**-" run at full speed over a short distance."
13. **Alias**-" used to indicate that a named person is also known or more familiar under another specified name."
14. **Exhaustion**- "state of extreme physical or mental fatigue."
15. **Stalking**- "pursue or approach stealthily."

My Mama Always Told Me…

High school once I finally started to learn to comb my own hair!

My Mama Always Told Me...

Chapter 8

Bully beatdown

My mom had been married many times as I recall. This one husband in **particular** was a mean and **irritable** dude and he was obviously no longer my mamas' favorite guy because while living with us she had another dude move in.
(Savage, I know!) She had been with him before I was even born to the point the dude thought I was his child!

My mama was **fearless** like that… All her men "friends" were cool with each other and everyone appeared to get along although they were all sprung over my mama. That's sexy Sandie if you didn't already know! 😊
I remember coming home from school one day and my mother was sitting in the living room smoking a cigarette and sipping on an Old English as usual, but on this day, she was crying. I asked her what was wrong, and she told me to go to my room.

I went to my room but of course stuck my ear to the door

to hear what was going on. According to the adult's **conversation,** my niece had reported to her school counselor that my mother's ex-husband had touched her **inappropriately.** Apparently, they did what's called a rape kit and discovered that my 7-year-old niece had been raped and they found semen traces to prove this. So, my family members, not to mention any names, decided that as soon as the **perpetrator** got home from work it was about to go down!

Let's just say all I could remember was loud music playing, fighting, and screaming right in my living room but aside from that typical fighting and screaming, I was used to this. Sounded like somebody was getting ready to die. Why did I look out my bedroom door and see a hammer being slung across his face? I couldn't erase that visual from my mind if I even wanted to. After everything "calmed down" so to speak and the music was turned off and the screams went away, I peeked out my door to see if anybody was around. There wasn't a person in sight!

There was blood everywhere, so I quickly slipped out the front door and walked to the corner store near my house. I went and bought some candy and hung out in the front of the store. I don't know for what, I just couldn't go home. I was pretty **traumatized** from what I had just witnessed, and an older man approached me. He asked me if I was ok and I told him no.

He invited me to his house, and you know that fearless side of me didn't see any issues with going to a stranger's house in the middle of the night, on a school night at that!

My Mama Always Told Me...

I walked a few blocks in the opposite direction from my house and wound up not far from my school. I had no clue if I would be comfortable to stay the night or what? But he made everything pretty comfortable for me. I told him most of what happened that night and he expressed that old boy was lucky because had it been his niece or daughter, he would have killed him!

He asked me if I wanted to go lay down in the bed and I told him that I could just chill on the couch. He **repeatedly** told me how pretty I was and how I had a nice smile. "I love that gap," he would say. He **insisted** that I come lay on the bed with him and I didn't want any trouble, so I **obeyed** his order. **Interesting** enough that we were just talking about my niece getting raped and this grown man is asking me to come lay in his bed with him; but, that's neither here nor there, I guess. He asked me how old I was, and I told him I was 14. (For sure he would lose interest at this point I thought).

Then he asked if I was a virgin and I expressed to him that I was. That was like a light bulb that went off in his head because instantly after, he started to kiss, rub and touch all over me. (Thinking to myself bruh, I just told you I was only 14!!) I asked him if he could stop because I just wasn't in the mood to be **affectionate** with anyone and he did. I lay there thinking that maybe it was time for me to go back home but I was afraid to do so.

He came closer and closer to me to the point where he was laying in between my legs and basically **dry humping** me... I lay there and didn't move because I was hoping maybe if he "finished" then it would all be over.

However, he just kept going on and on. I could smell the liquor on his breath, and I could tell that he was **intoxicated.** Finally, he **climaxed** and rolled off of me. As soon as he went to sleep, I got my things and I hurried up and walked back to my house!

I remember walking in, and blood being **splattered** all over the walls and all over the furniture. I walked into my room and shut the door behind me. I felt so sad for my niece because unfortunately she wasn't protected. I even thought to myself, "that could have been me." She stayed with us more than she stayed with her mother aka my sister who became a mom at a very young age! My mom basically helped take care of my niece for most of her younger life. She definitely drew the short end of the stick when it came to my sister's kids. She was treated very badly and everyone in the family felt sorry for her.

The next morning, I remember heading out to go to school and I saw my mom's ex-husband cleaning up his own blood etc. off the walls and off the furniture. I don't know what kind of person would do that to a child but I wanted him to get arrested but soon after that, he **disappeared** and never returned. I hoped that my niece would be able to get through this situation and receive help, but I don't think she ever did.

Not long after she went into the Foster care system, she didn't make the best choices with her life: running the streets, running away from homes, **disappearing** with all sorts of drugs etc. and being **promiscuous.** But now she is married with children and she has created a better life for herself. I'm very proud of her for this! I hope that she will protect her children better than anyone was able to protect her.

Poem

If I could have protected you there is no question to ask
Like an annoying little sister, I would brush you off to pass
If only I could change the activities that took place I would have
Repetitive generational curses left a long history of hurt and a sense of uttered sadness
My first chance at being a fill in parent but unapparent that I had
Too young to realize the impact and representation I had to be transparent
Teenage troubles never left a more solitude of what not to inherit
I wish I could have been made over to come and save you
This day replays over and over again answers in lieu
I'm forever in your corner and forever in debt to you
They say don't live your life with regrets
But now I find myself checking on my own throughout the night
Ready and willing for the most brutal of all fights
Protect and serve like the authorities just to ensure their alright
The innocents of all the children a constant highlight
I pray God protects your heart and ensures you a fresh new start
I'm rooting for you every step of the way reach for the stars so what if you hit Mars

Vocabulary

1. **Particular**- "used to single out an individual member of a specified group or class."
2. **Irritable**- "having or showing a tendency to be easily annoyed or made angry."
3. **Fearless**- "lacking fear."
4. **Conversation**- "a talk, especially an informal one, between two or more people, in which news and ideas are exchanged."
5. **Inappropriately**- "in a manner that is not suitable or proper in the circumstances."
6. **Perpetrator**- "a person who carries out a harmful, illegal, or immoral act."
7. **Traumatized**- "subject to lasting shock as a result of an emotionally disturbing experience or physical injury."
8. **Approached**- "come near or nearer to (someone or something) in distance or time."
9. **Insisted**- "demand something forcefully, not accepting refusal."
10. **Interesting**- "arousing curiosity or interest; holding or catching the attention."
11. **Obeyed**- "comply with the command, direction, or request of (a person or a law); submit to the authority of."
12. **Affectionate**- "readily feeling or showing fondness or tenderness."
13. **Dry humping**- "simulates sexual intercourse with (someone)."
14. **Intoxicated**- "(of alcoholic drink or a drug) cause (someone) to lose control of their faculties or behavior."
15. **Climax**- "the most intense, exciting, or important point of something; a culmination or apex."
16. **Promiscuous**- "having or characterized by many transient sexual relationships."
17. **Repeatedly**- "over and over again; constantly."

My Mama Always Told Me...

I stayed in my room, no reason to ever leave.

Chapter 9

An unforgettable trip

My first job I worked at a local fast-food restaurant. I was 15 years old and I was pretty good at my job to the point where when new people got hired on, my manager would allow me to train the newbies, as we called them. This dark chocolate fella began on a Friday and I remember it was odd since typically new folks started on Mondays.

I showed him a few tips and of course with the switch of my hips, he noticed me and asked for my number. He told me he lived in a **work release** which I knew was a place that guys who got out of jail or **correctional facilities** would live as long as they were working somewhere for a certain amount of time. He wasn't that good at his job I could tell firsthand, but I mean how hard was it to pour fries into a basket and drop into piping hot grease?

He would do goofy stuff like pour fries on the side of the basket and we would have to fish the fries out. I would get super irritated and **annoyed,** but he was so freaking cute! I couldn't help not being mad at him for long. He **flirted** with me all the time and he always asked if I had a boyfriend and at that time, I probably did! But it didn't matter because he was fine. And I knew if I wanted him, I could have him!

He was my "at work Bae", and we were always working the same shift so he helped to pass the time by, and I was making money so I couldn't complain. We never really hung out, outside from work but one day he was getting ready to miss **curfew** and asked me if I could take him home. I wasn't even supposed to be driving around like that because technically I didn't have my driver's license yet.

My mom gave me clear **instructions** to drive to work and back and that was it! But I gave him a ride because I felt sorry for him. (I did that a lot, went against what my mama said because the compassion I had for helping people even if it meant I could get in trouble.) Before he got out of the car, he said he had 10 minutes before he would be late and asked if I wanted to talk. He began telling me about his upbringing of selling drugs because his mother was an addict and could not take care of his younger siblings, so he had to help out all the time!

I felt bad for the **predicament** he was in at such a young age (16) so anytime he needed me I made sure to be there for him. He stopped coming to work a few weeks later, and as time went by, I didn't hear from him. He even missed my 16th birthday! I got my license and could freely dip out if I wanted to now and my mama couldn't say much to me at this point.

One day out the clear blue sky I got a call from him asking me if I had a boyfriend. (He was random like that!) I never mentioned one to him before, so we began to have what you call a long-distance relationship. He lived in Bremerton and he would call me every day and run game, which I knew better, but I guess I didn't care. He seemed like a cool dude and I enjoyed getting to know him until this one day I got a call late at night and after not hearing from him for about a week this time, he had a huge request of me. (I should have known.)

He sounded excited when we spoke and told me he needed me. (I loved being needed.). He said he and his cousin had to get to Bremerton, which was not right around the corner from Tacoma; and, he would come pick me up and I would have to take him and his cousin home. He said he had a vehicle (which surprised me!) but they just needed someone with l's aka a license and they had been drinking. So, I agreed that if he picked me up from my house that I would go with them and I would drive them to Bremerton, which was a good 30 to 45-minute drive.

He showed up blasting music outside my house, which was a complete no-no especially with my "crazy mama!" I got in the passenger seat and immediately turned the music down. He flashed for me to get in the driver's seat! He and his cousin sat in the back-blowing trees and I began to feel like a dang **chauffeur**! I had an attitude 20 minutes into the long ride to Bremerton. He stumbled up into the front seat next to me and began to rub on my leg and tell me how much he appreciated me rescuing him.

I could smell the alcohol and chronic reeking from his mouth. I was hoping that the police didn't pull us over because we're all young folks riding down the freeway all the way to Bremerton! He had this old raggedy van and he offered to give me a beer and I declined. I gave him the coldest shoulder. I was irritated because it was late at night and I'm driving him all the way to another town.

We got to his family's house and he introduced me to his aunt and his cousins who were little girls. We all hung out for a little bit because he went and passed out in the next room. The next day he told me his aunt would take me home. I don't think the aunt knew this though because when I mentioned it to her, she told me she had to work! Another day went by and I asked him if he could ask her for me to get a ride home and there was always an excuse as to why his aunt couldn't take me home.

After three (3) days of being there and finally realizing that I was stuck, I called my mama and told her where I was. She fussed and yelled at me, telling me that I was gonna have to figure out a way to get home since I decided to go all the way to Bremerton with some boys tryna be grown. Boy I got tired of hearing this, and I couldn't wait to be grown!

My boyfriend wanted to do some freaky things and I told him that I was NOT going to disrespect his aunt's house!

(Even though I would disrespect my mamas.) A few hours later his cousin made a pass at me and tried to lure me into the back room. I told my boyfriend and his response was, "Ain't no fun, if the homies can't have none!" (I found a lot of guys had that mentality at that age.) However, for the females who did partake in sleeping with their boyfriends' friends they would talk crazy about them, and they would be looked down upon!

It came the night when I put my foot down and finally expressed to my boyfriend that I wanted to go home, and he and his cousin volunteered to take me. I should have known something was weird when his aunt told me to come in her room to talk and she gave me a pocketknife! She told me if I needed to use it to do what I had to do! I got in the car with the boys and we proceeded to drive, and they took me to someone else's house and picked up two other females.

The females got in and I could instantly tell that it was some kind of double date going on here. I had a major attitude, I thought, "The nerve of this negro, swooping two chicks while I'm in his presence!" We pulled up to a gas station and they put gas in the vehicle and told me to get out! I told them, "You got me bent if you think you 'bout to just leave me on the side of the road thousands of miles away from home!" I was being set up! I was 40 minutes away from my home.

I told them that I was going to call the police if they didn't take me home and things got pretty violent! The cousin attacked me and bit me in my face, so I defended myself by cutting him with that little raggedy pocketknife and eventually they threw me out of the car! I was hoping the girls that they were with them would have helped me or said something to them, but they drove off and left me on the side of the road.

I called my mom and she called an officer to come pick me up. I was taken to a local shelter for teenagers and my mom and my boyfriend's mom had to come pick me up. I truly thank God that I was not hurt badly, and I was able to learn to not go places with people I didn't fully trust because anything could have happened. This dude was a convicted felon at age 16 and he clearly lived a lifestyle of running the streets and **demoralizing** women.

Poem

Don't trust them if they say
I was gonna call you anyway
Don't trust them when they say
How did you know what I liked to play?
Playing games and choosing names
Don't trust them when they say
I liked you from the moment I laid eyes your way
Don't trust them when they say
You're more beautiful today than yesterday
Don't trust them when they say
I could have any girl my way
When they try to run game and think without them, you'd go insane
All that talk just comes off so **mundane**
Don't trust them when they say
I been thinking about you all day
Pretending like they didn't just hang up with another
The whole time tryna act undercover
Don't trust them when they say
I think your so **fascinating**
Run far far away if they come at you talking this way

West coast for life! Hahaha
Finally got my own car! Bought and paid for!

Vocabulary

1. **Work release**- "leave of absence from prison by day enabling a prisoner to continue in normal employment."
2. **Correctional facility**- "prison, also known as a correctional facility, jail, penitentiary, detention center, correctional center, or remand center, is a facility in which inmates are forcibly confined and denied a variety of freedoms under the authority of the state."
3. **Annoyed**- "slightly angry; irritated."
4. **Flirted**- "behave as though attracted to or trying to attract someone, but for amusement rather than with serious intentions."
5. **Curfew**- "a regulation requiring people to remain indoors between specified hours, typically at night."
6. **Instructions**- "detailed information telling how something should be done, operated, or assembled."
7. **Predicament**- "difficult, unpleasant, or embarrassing situation."
8. **Chauffeur**- "a person employed to drive a private or rented automobile."
9. **Mundane**- "lacking interest or excitement; dull."
10. **Fascinating**- "extremely interesting."

My Mama Always Told Me…

Chapter 10

The Chat line part 1

I began working at age 15, my **Sophomore** year in high school. Not long after I began my **venture** into the work force field, I started saving for my first car. Within a few months my mom took me to the auction in our local town and I bought my very first car. Once I got out on the road you couldn't tell me nothing! I was driving all over town and sometimes even out of town whenever I had the opportunity to.

A few friends told me about a **chat line** that you could call in to and talk to people in the local city. I guess you could say it was an easier way of getting to know people without having to see them face-to-face. I talked to a few different guys here and there but one who lived in Seattle struck my interest more than others... We spoke on the phone every day for about two (2) weeks and he would always ask me to come and see him.

At the time I guess you could say I was playing hard to get (which I did a lot!) because although I would be in his town sometimes hanging out or going to visit my grandmother (Rest in paradise Granny) I just wasn't ready to meet him face-to-face yet. You could say I was insecure because I was overweight, and I didn't know how he would react to seeing me and my big ole thighs! So, I waited until he was completely interested in me and I made plans with him to go on a date. I drove all the way to Seattle from Tacoma (30 minutes plus) and I met up with him at a local restaurant.

He told me what he was wearing so that I would be able to spot him in the crowd of people, and when I saw him, I guess I was pleased for the most part. Although he wasn't quite what he expressed over the phone. He was a tad bit shorter than I recalled him saying and his attire was a bit shabby for my taste in guys, but his personality struck me as a cool individual. We sat down over dinner and we talked, and he asked me about the type of work that I did and how long it would be until I graduated from high school.

I wasn't too keen on the **conversation;** honestly, I was a bit bored, but he was paying for dinner, so I guess I didn't put up a big fuss. He put his hand on my leg and with grace I would brush it off in the form of a yawn. I did that about 3 or 4 times because I really didn't like to be touched. After dinner he asked if I wanted to go hang out at one of the local parks and I agreed against my better judgment. We went to some random hood-looking park and there weren't very many cars near the vicinity.

He asked me if he could kiss me. At first, I was like "nah I'm not ready for all that" but after talking a bit more I decided to go ahead and let him kiss me. The kissing turned into rubbing and the rubbing turned into extensive touching and before I knew it, he was all over me. I pushed him off and told him that I was getting ready to start heading home. He expressed to me, "why would you drive all the way to Seattle and not want to do anything freaky?"

I said to him that our first time meeting I was not going to be "getting down" with him like that! He became very aggressive and angry! He started tugging at my pants and trying to rip off my shirt! I yelled for help and he smacked me in the face! He pushed my seat back and climbed on top of me! He completely became another person and he fought me to remove my pants! He began thrusting over and over, but he wasn't even inside of me! I just remember yelling as loud as I could for someone to help me! He climaxed after about 3 minutes and climbed off me. My car had a cup holder and I remember him hammering down on it with his fist breaking it into pieces! Not only was I shocked but also, I was fearful that he would take his anger out on my face again.

I began to cry even more and begged him to let me drop him off at home so that I could go back to town before it got too late and my mother started to worry. We drove over to a local corner store because he had **promised** to get me some gas. He could see that my car was on empty! I told him I needed gas before I could go back to

Tacoma and he offered to put ten funky bucks in my gas tank. As soon as he got out of the car and finished pumping the gas, I locked the doors and hurried up and took off!

At the time I didn't have a cell phone so he would have been calling my house to try to get ahold of me and I hoped my mama didn't answer! By the time I got home I had 14 voicemails all from him yelling that he left his shoes in my car and he couldn't believe that I left him. I did not care about returning his shoes nor would I ever drive down to see him again after the behavior he displayed in my car.

I am very thankful that I didn't get hurt worse than what I did. I regret not contacting the authorities after he tried to rape me! I didn't know what they would say since he never actually entered my body. I told myself to stay off the chat line for a while because I saw for myself that people are crazy and will do anything and everything to harm you and get what they want!

Poem

This dude ain't no joke, my car was now broke
I swear I almost choked, yelling and gasping for some hope!
He left a feeling of **resentment**, mama always told me give **consent**
An immense turn of **endearment**, turned into a fear of **incoherent**
When we first met, he was cool, we both talked about school
He seemed like a pretty smart dude, but his anger took a turn of abuse
I never even saw this mess coming; he didn't fit the **description** of someone
Who would harm me, they say "never judge a book by its cover?"
That goes both ways cuz folks be undercover
How'd I get myself into this mess again? I thought
Fast tale little girl thinking I can be bought!
Boy the choices I made I took major risk
I'm lucky he didn't pull out his fist!
Its worse nowadays kids are getting snatched
Little girls walking around talking 'bout he looks like a snack!
Take it from me little mama you don't want that attack
Cuz once you caught up ain't no turning back!

Vocabulary

1. **Sophomore**- "a second-year college or high school student"
2. **venture**- "a risky or daring journey or undertaking"
3. **chat line**- "the access to, or connection with, a chat room"
4. **conversation**- "a talk, especially an informal one, between two or more people, in which news and ideas are exchanged"
5. **promised**- "give good grounds for expecting (a particular occurrence or situation)"
6. **resentment**- "bitter indignation at having been treated unfairly"
7. **consent**- "permission for something to happen or agreement to do something"
8. **endearment**- "a word or phrase expressing love or affection."
9. **incoherent**- "expressed in an incomprehensible or confusing way; unclear"
10. **description**- "a spoken or written representation or account of a person, object, or event"

Chapter 11

The chat line unfortunate part 2

A few months passed by from my first experience with the chat line and my friend told me about a new one! You would have thought I learned my lesson from the first time, but I was a hard head little girl my mama always told me remember? I thought this was different because it was only supposed to be for teenagers! We would talk to boys from all over the United States and some also from our local city. One day I met a guy on the chat line who said that he was 16. He said that he lived in Federal Way and that he wanted to meet me in person.

We spoke for a few weeks and I decided to go to see him and link up! I learned from previous mistakes of going and meeting people alone and this time I decided to bring my friend with me. We met at a local beach and when I got out of the car, I sent him a message to let him know what I was wearing and soon after sending him the message this guy approached me. My friend was standing right next to me and the guy asked me if we could speak in private without my friend right next to me.

I told my friend to wait for me in the car cuz after I peeped old boy, I knew this wasn't gonna take long! She told me if I needed anything to yell or scream her name! I looked at him and I said, "First of all, you are NOT 16!"

He said, "Oh yeah I know." He said, "I don't like telling people my real age!" (Weirdo! I thought!)

We sat down at the beach and we talked, and he put his hand on my thigh and began to rub up and down. I brushed his hand off my leg! He looked at me and said, "Oh it's like that?" I ignored him. All of a sudden, he whipped out this photo album of women that apparently, he had been "taking care of." He showed me pictures of them where they were laying on a bed full of money and some of them were naked! Immediately it came to my mind that this guy must have been a PIMP!

He expressed how he took women all over the world to Las Vegas to New York to down south and he spoiled them. He told me that I was prettier than any of the other females that he had working for him and that I would probably make a lot of money. I laughed out loud! I had grown up with a good number of dudes in my family who were also pimps and at some point, in time, shoot I felt like a pimp my dang self! I had dudes buying me whatever I wanted, giving me money and completely spoiling me! I thought in my mind this guy must think I'm really stupid to let him pimp me out for his benefit and although I was a young girl, I was still very intelligent to know not to put myself in any position like that, period!

I have many women in my family who had done this type of work and they regretted it and they would always advise me against it, so I knew better! (The guy not only was missing one of his teeth in the front! So, I knew the ninja couldn't fight! Misplaced sentences or incomplete thought) But he was not at all what he expressed to be over the phone let alone he was definitely not 16 years old.

 I told him I would think about it so that I could get away from him and get to my car and told him I would call him later on. That day I blocked his number and I decided to stay off the chat lines for good! This was the second guy I had met off the chat line who thought he was going to fool me with the okie doke!

My Mama Always Told Me…

My Mama Always Told Me…

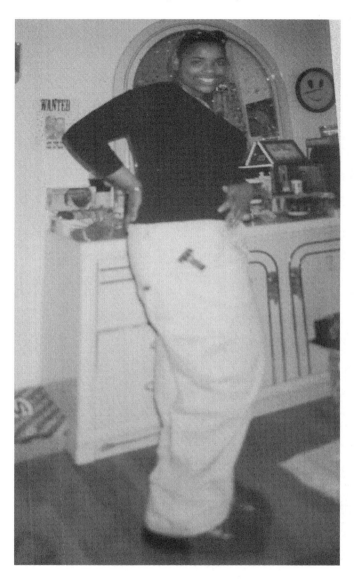

Poem

PYT (Pretty Young Thing)

He thought...
You're a pretty young thang, we can make a lot of money
Your skin is smooth and soft, I think I'll call you honey
Young and naive, they may think I am some dummy
But I curve 'em real quick leave 'em stuck and feelin' crummy
You ain't no pimp, and I ain't no ho.
I can get money without taking off my clothes
Not willing to **experiment**, even with them sorry **compliments**!
An **influencer** and **motivator** even at a young age.
All without having to get up on a stage.
An honest day's work worth more than your whole attitude
You must not know my daddy he already schooled me bout you dudes
Can spot 'em from a far, gazing out at the stars
Leaving females on stuck hopin' in and outta mens' cars
My **philosophy** taught me everything I know today
An **opportunity** even on days I may have forgot to kneel down to pray.
I spit the truth I've seen firsthand, if I ever pick that type of man
What comes with that territory trapped in the back of someone's van
Motel to Hotel in and out of the worst of worse if you can
Get out alive cuz some didn't make it, they tried to fake it and wound up in a ditch naked
Sad to say this is the truth, the picture had been painted

That street life ain't glitter and gold, walking up and down South Tacoma Way freezing cold
Loyal to those who do me right, **regardless** the struggles that may cause a fight
Nevertheless, my **experiences** created some pretty high stakes.
But chose me on that day, and I must say, the best decision I could ever make!

Vocabulary

1. **Influencer-** a person or thing that influences another"

2. **Motivator-** "something that provides a reason or stimulus to do something."

3. **Philosophy-** "study of the fundamental nature of knowledge, reality, and existence"

4. **Opportunity-** "a set of circumstances that makes it possible to do something

5. **Loyal-** "giving or showing firm and constant support or allegiance to a person or institution

6. **Regardless-** "without paying attention to a present situation; despite the prevailing circumstances"

7. **Nevertheless-** "in spite of that; notwithstanding; all the same"

8. **Experiences-** "practical contact with and observation of facts or events"

9. **Compliment-** "a polite expression of praise or admiration"

10. **Experiment-** "to determine something"

Chapter 12

Women can be something else!

My sister had this friend when I was in high school who tagged along with her everywhere, she went. Every time she came over, she would look at me and tell me how pretty I was and how I was such a sweetheart. (That's what everyone thought!) One day she came over and my sister wasn't home yet, so she decided to wait in our living room.

I don't know why she came to my house though. My sister had not lived with us since she was about 14 years old! But she kept asking me if I had a boyfriend and if I liked boys. I told her that I did and of course that I liked boys! She asked me if I ever thought about dating a girl? My response was "heck naw!"

I remember the look on her face as if I had **offended** her and at the time it was **taboo** for girls to like girls and boys to like boys (at least in my circle of friends!).

She asked me how old I was, and I replied that I was 16. Her response was, "dang girl you are thick for only 16 years old!" I got tired hearing this!

I didn't know what to make of that. It seemed pretty weird for a female to be commenting on what I looked like. I was used to hearing things like this from boys but never from a female! She asked me if I would ever be interested in kissing a girl and I told her "I'm good."

"Why not?" she said.

She kept **interrogating** me and I told her that I will call my sister to see how far she was because I was totally **uncomfortable** with the **conversation!** I wanted her to hurry up and get up out of my house! Eventually my sister showed up and I went into my room and closed the door behind me.

I knew that my sister and her probably had something going on more than what they let be known but I don't know for sure. Over time I found that my sister dabbled playing for the other team and I figured whatever floats her boat! None of my business!

The next day my sister asked me what she said to me while she was waiting for her to get back to the house. I told her what her friend was saying to me. She told me that was **uncalled for** and she shouldn't be talking to me like this period! My sister was a violent chick! She was not afraid of NOBODY including my mama and everybody was afraid of my mama! So, I told her not to worry about it, because I didn't want her to beat her little friend up over little ole me.

After a few days passed, the friend came over again without my sister being there (Unannounced!) asking if I knew when she would be home? I replied, "You know she doesn't live here right?"

She said "Yeah, but I like seeing you though!" Immediately after she said that I told her I would call her to figure out where she was! ☹ She then told me to come and sit next to her on the couch. I was raised to be **respectful** to adults and not be rude in any way, form or fashion, so I did what she asked.

At the time I had braids, and my sister's friend asked how long I had them done for? She wrapped a braid around her finger, twirling it around and around in circles. I knew she was totally coming on to me and I asked her to stop! She got closer and closer to me and leaned towards my face to try and kiss me. I put my hand up blocking her with the famous Martin (Errrrrrk!) her lips were coming for me!

I questioned "what the heck are you doing?"

She expressed to me that "girls kiss better than boys!" and she wanted to show me!

I told her, "I don't get down like that!" She persisted to get closer to me, **practically** pulling me closer and closer to her. For a little chick she was pretty strong! I decided to get up and go call my sister, but her phone was going straight to voicemail. I told her friend I felt like she should leave, and she replied back "I'm not going nowhere." I called my mom on the phone and got no answer.

"Where was these ninjas at?" I thought! I locked myself in my room and I stayed there until finally ole girl must've gotten tired of waiting and I heard her car start up and take off! I told my sister what **transpired**, and she told me to "stop lying." I **urged** her to believe me and she expressed "so in so ain't even like that!" I made sure any time her creepy friend came over I stayed in my room, took off to go hang out at one of my friends or something to avoid her at all cost. It wasn't long before she and my sister got into it and stopped speaking to each other and I never had to see her after that!

Girls feel like they are exempt from being pushed up on by members of the same sex. However, if we stand for something and we believe it whole heartedly we should not be afraid or closed mouthed about our beliefs. I feel as though young girls are targeted by women just as much as they are by men. We have a duty to protect them from this just as much as we would protect them from a grown man,

Poem

Listen to me will ya, why would I even lie?
I don't know what's going on here, but I definitely need an **alibi**
This chick must think I'm stupid; I don't get down that way
She came on real strong I'm telling you I had to **constantly** look in **dismay**
To think I would convert I'm sure would leave most of the men I knew hurt
I dated older dudes because I thought it would make me more mature?
But older women that one was new, I didn't even know what to do?
I couldn't even talk to my sis after that the type of folks you got up under you!
I was used to her dealing with scum bucket men and scumbags too
The females she hung with were also a pretty triflin' crew!
But none of them tried to hit on me though that one was new to come through!
Where was my protection? I wanted to run in the opposite direction!
I said no with no **hesitation**! You won't convince me to go on that **destination**!
I literally had no **explanation**! This chick was thirsty, and she needed **hydration**!

My Mama Always Told Me…

Vocabulary

1. **Offended-** to cause dislike, anger, or vexation.
2. **Taboo-** banned on grounds of morality or taste.
3. **Interrogating-** to question formally and systematically
4. **Uncomfortable-** causing discomfort or annoyance
5. **Conversation-** oral exchange of sentiments, observations, opinions, ideas.
6. **Uncalled -** not asked for, invited, or told to come
7. **Respectful-** marked by or showing <u>respect</u> or deference
8. **Practically-** in a <u>practical</u> manner
9. **Transpired-** to be revealed: come to light
10. **Urged-** to present, advocate, or demand earnestly or pressingly
11. **Alibi-** an excuse usually intended to avert blame or punishment
12. **Constantly-** without variation, deviation, or change : ALWAYS
13. **Dismay-** to cause to lose courage or resolution
14. **Destination-** a place to which one is journeying to which something sent
15. **Hesitation-** a pausing or faltering in speech

My Mama Always Told Me...

Chapter 13

The laundry mat

My mom was considered to be a **gypsy**, so we moved around a lot! And when we landed in a place with no washer and dryer; boy did I get hot! I had to gather all my clothes and covers for a weekly visit to the "wash house" as we called it. And every time we went the owner would be **gawking** over at me every second of every minute! I felt so **uncomfortable** and never went alone.

Every week I would make a hangout spot of it calling any friend I had on the phone. One day the guy asked if I needed some extra quarters. He explained someone left them behind. My mama always told me not to take nothing from no dude because they would want something in return on the sly. I didn't have any **intentions** on **embarking** on no Usher Raymond "letting it burn." I told ole dude I had money and didn't need any of his, as my stomach churned. Said, "I had a job and could pay to wash my clothes on my own and no need for a handout but thanks for your concern."

He watched as I walked past, even followed me when I would go back and forth inside. I felt so **troublesome**, every now and then I would try and hide. I had to use the restroom one day and to my surprise no tissue paper. What could I say? I got his attention to inform him of such and requested he help a sista out. He rushed quickly to grab a roll and gave a big ole shout. I proceeded to the restroom needing to go really bad; a sense of urgency came over no doubt.

He followed me into the restroom and shut the door behind him, turning the lights out. He pushed me up against the wall hands mawing me as if we were in a **brawl**! He kissed my neck, grabbed my butt and thrust his groin. I tried to fight him off in hopes of dropping and crawling. He ripped my shirt, and scratched my chest **revealing** my breast. I thought, "God is this a test?" What could I do? He stood about 6'2", weighing about 222 wearing a men's size who? plus 2. I fought with all my strength and smacked his face, yelling "what a complete disgrace!"

I quickly ran out of there.
"Man, what a drastic scare, moved on with **despair.** He even messed up my hair." Left my clothes, **stumbling** all over my toes. He thought anything goes! I smiled at him just to be nice, and to my surprise he took that as an invitation to my thighs! Never again to return, I told all my friends they **threatened** if he ever tried to do it again that would most **certainly** be the end!

Poem

Travel in twos the old timers would say
Men will look at you like a lion eyeing his prey
No care in the world sometimes if they are discovered
Trying extremely hard to pretend to be undercover
When going out in the public this is the world we now live in
There's no telling what could happen and how it could spin
Imagine being in a situation you didn't think you would get out
But the ability to protect yourself will leave you even if you just shout
Be mindful of your surroundings and those who come into contact
Ensure you have someone with you that will have your back
That way in the event something happens you are quick to react
If you are uncomfortable in any situation or out of place to interact
Follow your first mind and don't think twice about a resolution to retract

My Mama Always Told Me…

Vocabulary

1. **Gawking-** a clumsy stupid person
2. **Intentions-** what one intends to do or bring about
3. **Embarking-** to make a start
4. **Troublesome-** giving trouble or anxiety : VEXATIOUS
5. **Revealing-** allowing a look at or understanding of something inner/hidden
6. **Brawl-** to quarrel or fight noisily : WRANGLE
7. **Despair-** a cause of hopelessness
8. **Stumbling-** to walk unsteadily or clumsily
9. **Threatened-** having an uncertain chance of continued survival
10. **Certainly-** it is certain that : ASSUREDLY

My Mama Always Told Me...

Chapter 14

My brother's friend

My mother started over with having kids. So, I have a brother who is 9 years older than me and my sister is 8 years older than me. My brother had a lot of male friends, mostly gang members and drug dealers who used to come to the house all the time! I remember the week before I turned 18 this guy came to the house and he saw me. He was an older "**gentleman**" and he looked at me and said "Dang, how old are you?"

"I will be 18 in a week!"
"Wow, I will be back in a week then!" he replied.

Sure enough, this dude showed up the day after my birthday and offered to take me out! I agreed although he was definitely not my type. He was a big chunky dude, tall and dingy looking! His **hygiene** was very poor, and he had the raggediest car ever! (I was hardly materialistic, but I wasn't trying to get clowned by the homies.)

He took me out. I suppose I had a decent time and he offered to take me shopping. I was old enough to buy my own clothes I told him, mainly because I knew he was the type of dude who didn't want something for nothing! I didn't need him to take me shopping especially if he expected to get something out of return. He expressed to me he didn't want anything from me but my company and that he felt like I could dress a little more mature for my age.

So, a few weeks went by and we hung out from time to time and one day I was driving in his car with him and he pulled in an alley and proceeded to touching himself. (Super **random**, I thought like "who does that?") I looked out the window in the opposite direction, shocked and surprised at this type of behavior! He then grabbed my hand and placed it on his private area and told me to touch him. I put my hand back in my lap and refused and he then took out his private and told me to put my mouth on it.

I tried to get out of the car, but he locked the doors and told me I wasn't going anywhere. He then proceeded to drive, and we ended up in Oregon, almost two (2) hours from where I lived! He took me to his mother's house and told me that he was going to take me shopping after he introduced me to his mother. I told him I didn't want to meet his mother because we weren't in a relationship!

I didn't see the point in meeting any of his family,

especially after he pulled the stunt that he did. Not to mention the ninja basically kidnapped me! I didn't ask or give my permission to drive to the next state! He was a drug dealer, this I knew, but what I didn't know was he was also "serving" his own mother with drugs! I thought this was the lowest of the low for a human being to poison their own parent with drugs.

I asked him to take me home and he refused. He stated that I was his girlfriend and I couldn't go anywhere without his permission! "Negro what!??" I thought. I was scared and I feared that he would hurt me if I tried to leave without his permission. I called my mom to see if she could come get me but at the time, she didn't have a car! I stayed there in that raggedy, **disgusting** house for two (2) days and then finally he decided to take me home.

Every night he would try to touch me and rub me, and I would squirm and wiggle away from him telling him I was menstruating! He would offer to "put a towel down!" I told him that was just **scandalous**! I would often lock myself in the bathroom to avoid being next to him. By this time, I was sexually active; however, I did not give it up to any and everybody, especially not him!

He tried to rough me up one night and "take it". I ended up having to knee him in the groin to keep him away from me! This upset him **tremendously** so he smacked me and pulled my hair, telling me if I ever did something like that again he would kill me! I begged him to take me home and I would leave him alone for good. When he dropped me off at home, I told my mom everything that happened, and she told me that's what the heck I got for being a fast tale little girl!

"Mama I'm 18 now!"

Her reply, "well then you know more than I do!" (Sometimes she could be so cold and brutal with her words!)

About a week later, one of my friends told me they saw him in the mall with some female going shopping and told him they were going to tell me about this **sighting.** He expressed that he was shopping for me. He came to my mom's house begging to speak to me and told me that he had clothes for me. I told him where he could take those clothes! I told him I never wanted to see him again and I **reiterated** the fact that he was violently aggressive with me and I should have called the police on him, but I didn't. I regret that because he should have had to pay for what he tried to do to me!

Poem

Black man as you stand and look in the mirror once again
How can you **pretend** that you're any kind of friend?
Putting your hands on a female once again
No respect, no morals or any code,
Get dark and ugly I see you as cold!

Selling drugs to your family and friends,
I view something less than any kind of man!
Don't let the stereotype supersede you,
Intellect drippin' and I see right through!
Heart as cold as ice proppin' up that pipe,
Jewelry women's clothes don't believe the hype!

This all comes with an **extensive** price,
Why can't you just do what's right?
The dope man's coming as they cheer from the stands,
Not realizing it's their loved one's family and friends!
Dying on the streets, attracted to the fast life,
Hesitant to change, settle down, have some kids after marrying your wife!

That would be too easy and complicated all rolled into one,
Paranoid and always reaching for a gun!
Coward mentality has been a constant struggle,
Some ninjas just don't know how to stay outta trouble!

My Mama Always Told Me…

Vocabulary

1. **Gentleman-** a man of noble or gentle birth
2. **Hygiene-** a science of the establishment and maintenance of health
3. **Random-** without definite aim, direction, rule, or method
4. **Disgusting-** causing a strong feeling of dislike or disinclination
5. **Scandalous-** offensive to propriety or morality : SHOCKING
6. **Sighting-** the process, power, or function of seeing
7. **Tremendously-** to a great or tremendous extent : EXTREMELY
8. **Reiterated-** to state or do over again or repeatedly
9. **Pretend-** to give a false appearance of being, possessing, or performing
10. **Extensive-** having wide or considerable extent

My Mama Always Told Me...

Chapter 15

No means N to the O!

I dated this guy on and off for about six (6) years. Some would have called him my middle school and high school sweetheart, although I had other boyfriends **intermittently**. We never had sex and I guess you can say I was saving myself for marriage. (Clearly that didn't happen, unfortunately). So, we became older and had multiple "almost" **interactions,** but I could never bring myself to go further with him. It was just something about him my spirit could not completely trust.

I had this boyfriend who actually turned out to be one of this guy's friends. (Never thought I would be that girl!) My boyfriend went out of town one weekend and my ex decided to invite himself over to hang out with me at my apartment. The ex knew my boyfriend was out of town and he couldn't have picked a worse time to come because we had been arguing for a few days prior. (Maybe it was a setup?)

I guess I didn't see the harm in allowing him to come over and watch a few movies, perhaps hang out and talk about old times. He called me from outside to let me know he was downstairs, so I invited him to come up to my apartment. When he came in, he gave me a big ole hug and made himself comfortable on my living room couch. He was a big dude, so I hoped he didn't leave an imprint on the dag blasted couch! We watched two movies and he began to get comfortable. He asked if he could lay in my room on my bed.

We had been on and off for so many years, but I really felt bad about knowingly cheating on my boyfriend. He was a good dude and I thought he deserved better than that! So, I decided to send him a text breaking up with him (as if this would make my conscience clear) but it didn't! I then turned my phone off in order to not be disturbed, and ole boy began kissing me all over and I decided to kiss him back. As time **progressed** clothes were removed and he ended up on top of me.

He peeked around in the dark, so to speak, and before he would enter my body, I asked him to stop! Maybe I had a change of heart about my boyfriend, or the guilt set in that I should not be doing this! He continued to try and guide himself and I blurted out again to stop. I tried to push him off me, but he was twice as big as I was, and he **persisted** and found his way inside of me as he thrusted and pushed his way. I began to cry and every emotion including anger, rage, fear, and sadness took over me.

He didn't even bother to put on any protection, which made me even more upset because I already had a child. I wasn't trying to get pregnant again, nor was I trying to contract any diseases from having unprotected sex! Not long after the jerk started, he then finished. He rolled off me and asked me if I was on birth control. I **sobbed** for a moment and quietly told him no and then he asked me if I could go get a plan B pill which he offered to pay for.

I thought to myself if he would have stopped in the first place as I asked him to we wouldn't be in this type of **predicament**. I didn't even know what a plan B pill was. I have never taken one before! I asked him to leave my apartment and with no **hesitation** he found his way to the door! I turned my phone back on instantly after I closed and locked my front door, then I texted him to never call or come by my apartment again!

What I should have done was listen to my spirit that clearly knew this guy was a dirtbag! I should have never allowed him to come over, especially with my boyfriend being out of town and I put myself in a **defenseless** position. I **exposed** a part of me he felt was weak and he took **advantage** of me. Sometimes we must just go with that gut feeling that tells us what our mind may not be thinking, that's why it's called **intuition**. That hunch or **instinct** to have the **discernment** to make the right decision should not be looked pass.

Poem

I told him to stop, right after he laid on top
He made his way to get all hot and my insides felt like they could rot!
I guess one would say, well you invited him over
What did you think you were clean and **sober**?

But I didn't think! That's the problem!
Always trying to solve someone else's problem?
Not **realizing** I'm creating all these problems!
Resulting in an even bigger problem!!

I take ownership of the situation nonetheless,
Allowing this man to fondle my breasts!
I welcomed the attention and the **affection**,
Not considering this man may get an erection!

Inconsiderate to my partner's feelings,
Praying God can give us all healing!
Being more careful and responsible with my body,
Not to play with life like it's just a hobby!

Vocabulary

1. **Intermittently-** coming and going at <u>intervals</u> : not continuous
2. **Interactions-** mutual or reciprocal action or influence
3. **Progressed-** a forward or onward movement to advance
4. **Persisted-** to be insistent in the repetition or pressing of an utterance
5. **Sobbed-** to cry or weep with convulsive catching of the breath
6. **Predicament-** a difficult, perplexing, or trying situation
7. **Hesitation-** a pausing or faltering in speech
8. **Defenseless-** lack of means or method of defending or protecting oneself, one's team, or another
9. **Advantage-** a factor or circumstance of benefit to its possessor
10. **Exposed-** open to view-- not shielded or protected
11. **Intuition-** immediate apprehension or cognition
12. **Discernment-** the quality of being able to <u>grasp</u> and comprehend what is obscure
13. **Sober-** abstaining from drinking alcohol or taking intoxicating drugs
14. **Realizing-** to bring into concrete existence
15. **Affection-** a feeling of liking and caring for someone or something: tender attachment

I learned to smile through the pain and disappointment.
#Smiley

Chapter 16

"My Stepdaddy ain't no good"

My mama's fourth (4th) husband was a real jerk! I remember he treated her like crap, and he stepped out on her a lot. He was always very rude to me and because I had a lot of boyfriends (guys for friends) he would always say some slick mess like… "You sure do have a lot of dudes running in and out of this house!" Little did he know I wasn't even fooling around with anybody! When I got to high school I couldn't wait until I could be gone all day to avoid him at all cost.

He gave me a **bad vibe** ever since I caught him and my mama **fooling around** when I was a younger kid. I literally only had time to go to school, work and sleep. My social life diminished drastically. At work we got a new manager and one week she totally jacked up the schedule. She didn't add me to the weekend shift and for once in a long time I had the weekend off. I didn't want to complain so I just went with the flow of things. I called up some of the homies and invited them to go "joy riding" with me around town.

My car was fairly small, but we made it work. After a day of hanging out I invited my homeboys to come hang out at my house. Although I knew my mom wasn't home, I literally had no interest in these dudes, they were strictly buddies of mine. Plus, my mom knew both of these dudes and she **adored** them both! We sat up in my room watching television and cracking jokes back and forth. Next thing I knew my bedroom door had been pounded on repeatedly.

I don't know if we were laughing too loud or what, but it was my mom's husband coming to **impose** on the fun again. He began yelling out obscenities about me moaning and groaning and called me every name in the book. "You dirty little whore!" he yelled out first. One of my homeboys stated "Sandie, you want me to drop that foo?" And I expressed to him NO!! I knew he was either drunk or high from the boldness of him beating on my door. I unlocked my door (yes, my mama gave me the room with the deadbolt on the door) and I told my friends we were leaving!

Her husband continued to yell calling me a little tramp and **insinuating** I was having a threesome with my two homeboys and all I could do was laugh. I did that a lot, laughed out of **nervousness** or what have you because crying was just not an option. He followed me to the car fussing and yelling and finally I got in the car with the fellas and it took every bit of me to avoid running him over with my car! I called my mom from my friend's house and told her what had just taken place. She expressed that he was probably **intoxicated** (as if this is supposed to excuse the behavior).

I returned home late that night and when I came into the house everything was dark and dim; it seemed as if no one was home. I went to my room and my door was cracked open. I peeked my head in the door and this dude was sitting on my bed! I respectfully asked him to get up out of my room and he **motioned** for me to come sit next to him on my bed. I yelled for my mom, but she didn't answer. I went to walk toward her room, and he jumped up and shut and locked my door.

I told him I would scream if he touched me and he informed me that no one was home. I could tell that he and my mom must have gotten into it because he had a few scratches on his arms and face. He pushed his body closer and closer to mine, each time I backed away more and more. I asked him what he wanted, and he said, "baby girl I wanna apologize." I got used to getting called names and being accused of being a fast-little girl ever since I was a little girl so at this point, I was numb to the name-calling.

I shrugged my shoulders and told him to forget about it, then he expressed he wanted to make it up to me. I told him that was ok, and he insisted I tell him what I wanted. Because he thought I was some promiscuous little girl I told him I wanted some money! He asked me how much and I knew he was a **contractor** for the military, so I know he had bread and butter! I told him to give me $100 and he agreed. My house phone had been ringing off the hook, but he wouldn't let me pick it up! He stated "First, what are you gonna do for this $100?"

I looked at him and he was grabbing his private area looking me up and down! I **bolted** towards the door and he reminded me that no one was home; and, if he wanted it, he would just take it but he was willing to pay for it.

I told him I was not a ho and I did not sleep with dudes for money. He then blurted out, "Oh you do it for free then!" He pushed me on the bed and started unbuckling his pants and I laid there hoping my brother, or somebody would come home any minute before what I thought was about to happen, happened. He asked me again if I was going to "give it to him", or if he had to "take it!" I told him I was a virgin and had never had sex before and he expressed "that's ok baby girl, I will go slow!"

I'm thinking to myself like "What the heck does that even mean?" Within a few moments I heard the doorbell ring and I dodged past him and ran to the door. (Never had that much ability in all my days!) I opened the door without even asking whom it was and to my surprise my boyfriend was standing on the porch looking irritated! "Why ain't you been picking up the phone?" he yelled, and I hurried down the stairs with him and jumped in my car!

I drove to his house and told him I would explain once we got there. I told him and his mom what happened, and they encouraged me to stay at a friend's house for the next few days. I kept thinking to myself if my mama doesn't leave him, I'm moving out, and within a few weeks... that's exactly what I did! I moved out into my own apartment and never looked back. Not long after moving out my mama and this idiot got divorced and who knows where he ended up or with whom. I just hope that the person didn't have any young kids.

Poem

Supposed to be a role model and protector you were not
Accusing me of being some little fast tail t.h.o.t
I had so many friends and acquaintances who would have easily blew up his spot
However, the violent and anger that filled my chest left me more than hot
But not angry enough to retaliate causing a rift in the house which would end in a reckless thought
Protection of the secrets can eat away at you for ever and ever
The acts were not wise nor were they clever
I could have not done any different than that situation with each endeavor
Parents shield the children young and older
Never assume teenagers are strong or fearless
They are just as much in need of a safeguard
It's not like they want a swarm of folks to bombard
Yet the frequent check-in and not just your bank card

Vocabulary

1. Bad vibe- a distinctive negative feeling or quality capable of being sensed
2. Fooling around- to engage in casual sexual activity
3. Adored- to regard with loving admiration and devotion
4. Impose- to establish or bring about as if by force
5. Insinuating- winning favor and confidence by imperceptible degrees
6. Nervousness- appearing or acting unsteady, erratic, or irregular
7. Intoxicated- affected by alcohol or drugs especially to the point where physical and mental control is markedly diminished
8. Motioned- an act or instance of moving the body or its parts : GESTURE
9. Contractor- one that contracts to perform work or provide supplies
10. Bolted- to move or proceed rapidly-- to move suddenly or nervously

My Mama Always Told Me…

Chapter 17

All boy party

My mama was always lenient when it came to me hanging out with my friends and stuff. Every now and then I would go to "Kids clubs," or dances etc. I got invited to this house party one night and I told my mom I was going to Club Friday which was downtown Tacoma. Those of you from that era know Club Friday used to be crackin'! Some nights too much though, where a fight would break out or some idiot would shoot at or in the vicinity of the club.

No one ever got hurt that I know of but this particular Friday it was closed. Something must have happened so the homies decided to throw a house party! I had never been to a party at someone's house before. I mean I had birthday parties that were pretty turnt up, but this was different!

I remember one of my close homeboys and a few of the other guys I went to school with were there. I was a little worried once more and more dudes began to show up though. I was one to always show up early if not on time and as hour after hour went by, the girl to boy ratio **altered** quite a bit. I heard stories from middle school of boys running trains on girls. One of them happened to be my little puppy love and one of his homeboys.

I lost all respect for him after that, thinking "how could you disrespect a female like that?" But on the flip side, I guess she didn't have respect for herself either to let multiple boys "hit" **simultaneously**. I don't know how they got down nor was I interested in finding out.

A couple dudes I knew, but we weren't close or anything, were pointing and talking about me from the other side of the room. I was nervous as all get out, hoping they wouldn't approach me because I knew I was NOT going for the okie doke, as they used to say!

They continued to nod at me and wave from across the room and I sat up pretending like my pager was going off. I was supposed to be meeting one of my good homegirls at this party and she clearly was either running super late or was not going to show up. I asked the boy whose house we were kickin' it at if I could use his phone and he said to me "yeah but block the number out!"

Back in my day, when you didn't want someone to have your number you would first dial *69 and then dial the number. Now there's an app for that!

So, I called my friend and fussed at her for being late. She apologized **profusely** and **declared** she was waiting on her mother to get home from work, but she was dressed and ready to go! I asked why she didn't just take the bus? And of course, being in Washington it was raining, and she didn't want to get her hair wet! I told her I could have come and picked her up; and, I forgot my friend's mom was a **workaholic** like myself so she couldn't get off any earlier.

We chatted for a little bit, especially since I was wanting to avoid thing one and thing two over in the corner plotting on me. Finally, my friend yelled, "My mom's is here! I'm on my way!" I hung up the phone and went and sat back down. To my surprise (Not really) the two fellas **approached** me.

The one got really close to me and said, "Do you blow?" I swear I almost smacked him into next week! I shifted my whole body directly towards him (I was a bold one) and said, "Excuse me!?" With a surprised look he pulled out two blunts from his pocket.

I come from a long lineage of tree blowers, however... I was not one of them! I **retorted** with "I don't smoke!"

He asked why and we went back and forth. He tried to convince me that I was **uptight** and needed to relax and if I just took two hits, I would be cool.

I remember back in the 7th grade Bill Clinton admitting to hitting the weed but not inhaling; and, I didn't want to look like a complete L7, as they called me back then anyway (A square). So, I agreed to hit the weed, I just wasn't going to inhale! Ha! Little did I know, that was easier said than done. They directed me to come to one of the rooms in the back, and I inquired why we couldn't just do it right there in the living room. They expressed because the house didn't need to be smelling like **dro** when old boys' parents returned home.

Parents get cameras installed in your house right now! **Gullible** as they come, I followed dumb and dumber back to the room, we all sat on the bed and they lit up. Thing one hit it first, then thing two, then it was my turn… Ok, this was my acting **debut** and I had to put on a good show! A little cough here, a little gasp for air there and then pass it! So, I hit the blunt, and what I thought would appear to be viewed as me inhaling it did not go over very well.

I accidentally inhaled the dang thing! I just KNEW I was going to have a dang asthma attack! One of the dudes patted my back as I was coughing up my left lung, I'm sure of it! They both laughed **uncontrollably** and passed the blunt back around in what I guess they call a rotation. When it came back to me, I happily declined because you see I was already good and high! (My mother would be so proud, I thought.)

They insisted again so nervous and **distraught,** I took another hit trying really hard not to inhale this time. I held the smoke in my mouth for a few minutes then I figured instead of letting it come out of my mouth, I would do it like I did my nebulizer treatment sometimes when I was a kid pretending to smoke a cigarette and let it come out my nose. I unknowingly realized this was inhaling it too!

Lawd hammercy one mistake after another here! It was a wrap for me when I tell you I laid down on my back. I remember the one ugly one telling his homeboy to take off my pants. Old boy put the blunt out and he did what his buddy told him to do, and they took turns performing oral acts on me.

I was pretty **intoxicated**, so nothing was **pleasurable** to say the least. But I recall trying to scream for help and one of them covering my mouth with his hand. I recall the one pulling out his penis and trying to stick it in my mouth and I was high but not that high! So, I kept my mouth closed and would not open it not one little bit!

Next thing I know the one told him "If she's not gonna do it homie…" and he looked at him and got down on his knees with no hesitation! The other one grabbed my hand and wrapped it around his penis and forced me to rub and stroke it. "Was this a train?" I questioned?

I remember my friend busting in the room, helping me to put my pants on and calling a cab to get me home after that. The next day she called me and asked me "what the heck I was doing in that room?" I told her all I could remember was hitting the blunt! She fussed at me because she was a smoker and I wouldn't even smoke with her! I told her **peer pressure** is something else. She told me I was lucky they didn't rape me, and I felt the same way.

My Mama Always Told Me...

Poem

There was two of them, what was I supposed to do? They outnumbered me and I didn't know what they knew.
Convinced me to step out of character how insane Some would say I was gone in the brain.
Incoherent, incomprehensible, completely puzzled He tried to cover my mouth like a dog putting on a **muzzle**.

What was I thinking? Sitting here kicking myself. I needed help and not one person to come?
They were pretty lucky I thought, things didn't get overly hot. They don't know where I'm from!
Boy the mistakes we kids make, this one had to take the cake and not one I could say that I baked!
Sitting there worried as ever they really thought they were clever. I'm so glad my girl didn't flake!

Always travel in twos my mama taught me, cuz she knew my girls gotta be right there just in case of some trouble. You never know a person's **intentions**, and plus not to mention calling for help they would be there on the double!
Young kids just wanna have fun, and I get it. I was that one life of the party you could say, come through all day Terrible choices I made, always the one to get preyed on. Life's not always black and white, sometimes that mess is gray!

Who's to say that one day, my mistakes won't catch up to me and the worse I could imagine takes me away. Parents

keep tabs on your kids, I don't care if they get pissed, they'll be thanking you some say!
At times I hated my mom. I always thought she was wrong, now here I am singing this sad, sad song.
She knew more than I did, and I sat up being a spoiled kid doing all the things she forbid!

Vocabulary

1. Simultaneously- existing or occurring at the same time
2. Altered- made different in some way
3. Profusely- exhibiting great abundance
4. Declared- to make known formally, officially, or explicitly
5. Workaholic- a compulsive <u>worker</u>
6. Approached- to come very near to
7. Retorted- to answer (an argument) by a counter argument
8. Uptight- being tense, nervous, or uneasy
9. Gullible- easily duped or cheated
10. Debut- a first appearance
11. Uncontrollably- incapable of being controlled
12. Distraught- agitated with doubt or mental conflict or pain
13. Pleasurable- causing a feeling of <u>pleasure</u> or enjoyment
14. Peer pressure- a feeling that one must do the same things as other people of one's age and social group in order to be liked or respected by them
15. Convinced- to belief, consent, or a course of action
16. Incoherent- lacking normal clarity or intelligibility in speech or thought
17. Incomprehensible- impossible to comprehend -- having or subject to no limits
18. Muzzle- a fastening or covering for the mouth of an animal used to prevent eating or biting
19. Intentions- what one <u>intends</u> to do or bring about

My Mama Always Told Me...

Chapter 18

Just me and my boyfriend

When I was about 13, I met this boy in middle school. He was nothing short of a GANGSTA! He spoke whatever was on his mind and he ran the streets, taking whatever, he wanted from whomever he wanted to. We were **acquaintances** for many years, and he was a good friend to me. My sophomore year in high school I guess you could say I was in between boyfriends and he and I started "talking" as we used to say.

He was very intelligent and charismatic. He knew I was **multifaceted** and possessed many talents. And I knew if worse came to worse he had my back! He and I began dating and after a few months of purely kissing and rubbing I could tell he wanted more. I always felt like if the guys I dated weren't getting sex then they would get bored with me.

I don't know if that was true with him or not but after

another few months went by, he asked me if he could give me oral pleasures. Well, he said "let me eat you out." I guess I knew what that was, but I had never had that done before. I had a few dudes offer; one even did so but outside of my underwear.

I told my boyfriend that I wasn't going to do him if that was what he was thinking, and he expressed that was fine. I remember him removing my panties and first kissing my private parts really slowly. I laid there staring at the ceiling feeling completely **uncomfortable**.

In my mind this was still keeping my "virginity" but giving into my already experienced boyfriend. I knew he had sex before and I was unsure how to please him without having **intercourse**. Most of the women in my family were pretty young when they became sexually active and I was on a mission you could say to hold onto my **"innocence"** as long as I could.

Eventually (a few weeks went by) and I felt bad that he was the only one doing the "pleasuring." I decided to return the favor. I knew if my mama caught us, we were both going to get beat! I guess you could say he was my first love though. We would do anything and everything for each other. But we were definitely too young for sex or **intimate** acts.

A few months went by and he and I came to the house to hang out. I remember my mama telling us to go in the room and "make a baby!" I laughed hysterically as I did… and brushed her off because we were not having sex. Then I wondered if she was serious in saying this to us. She would always say we would make cute babies! And it made the both of us very nervous!!

Most of my siblings were under the age of 16 when they had their first child. My boyfriend was 16 and I was 15, but we were completely not interested in having any kids! I questioned if my mom thought we were having sex, why she didn't fuss or holler like she did before I started **experimenting** in the bedroom.

I got so used to being called a little fast tale girl and now she was welcoming that behavior? I know she really approved of my dude and I thought maybe that's why she was so comfortable? My mind was blown away and so was my boyfriends! But we never went forth with that level. Isn't that **interesting**, when someone wants you to do it, you lose interest all together?

My Mama Always Told Me…

Poem

My first love, I looked to you. **Sprung** wouldn't even begin to describe,
We walked around hand in hand, couldn't tell us nothin' and we did it with pride!
With respect and appreciation no matter the situation you know I had your back,
Our **commitment** to one another, at times would sometimes smother but we never
Wanted to hurt each other plus I loved that you were southern.

Just some kids from the Tac, if anyone stepped, they were bound to get attacked!
Remember that time at the high school cuttin' up like a fool,
You'd have called me a ghoul, so full of fuel everyone **witnessing** this Black girl rule!
We were so young and dumb, not knowing the **consequences** of so much fun
I didn't know you were packin' no gun, out all night on the run avoiding being outdone.

Everyone thought we would always be together, no regrets this ain't no love letter
I just wished that we both knew better, I guess you could say we were relationship goals like **trendsetters**.
Just some kids from the Tac, who had each other's back nothing wrong with that!
And anyone who doesn't understand, we vibed out no doubt **kindred spirits** alike
I was your **wombman** and you were my "man"

But we were just kids nothing more, many trips to the store we did adolescent stuff all the time
Should have waited, continued dating. You were always getting faded but respected I wasn't into that kind of stuff.
Some would say you were rough but respected my tough
You never tried to call my bluff!

You will always have a place in my heart, I think back to the start.
A true friendship you and I could not look past.
My ride or die as they say, for you I would always pray down til' this day.
You would always be right there to gas!

Vocabulary

1. **Multifaceted** - having many facets or aspects
2. **Kindred spirits-** of a similar nature or character
3. **Wombman-** having the ability to create and protect. life, both biologically and figuratively
4. **Trendsetters-** someone or something that starts or helps to popularize a new fashion, style, movement, etc.
5. **Consequences-** a conclusion derived through logic
6. **Witnessing-** one who has personal knowledge of something one that gives evidence
7. **Commitment-** an agreement or pledge to do something in the future
8. **Sprung-** Utterly infatuated with someone
9. **Interesting-** holding the attention : arousing interest
10. **Experimenting-** try out a new procedure, idea, or activity
11. **Intimate-** marked by a warm friendship developing through long association
12. **Innocence-** lack of knowledge-- freedom from guile or cunning
13. **Intercourse-** physical sexual contact between individuals that involves the genitalia of at least one person
14. **Uncomfortable-** causing discomfort or annoyance
15. **Acquaintances-** personal knowledge a person whom one knows but who is not a particularly close friend

Visiting my lil boyfriend at Maple Lane Correctional Facility.

Chapter 19

Oh, my virginity

The month before I turned 16, I lost my "virginity." That's how unenthused I was with the act; I don't even remember the date it happened. I had been dating this thug dude on/off for about 2-3 years. He went to an alternative school and was in and out of correctional facilities. He was quite the bad boy, which I kind of liked! The first time we hung out I remember skipping school and catching the bus over to his apartment.

His mom worked so she was gone that day. I remember he was blasting some Brotha Lynch as if that was romantic music for female company or something. He invited me in and before I knew it, we were completely naked underneath the blankets. I was nervous as I don't know what and told him that I had changed my mind.

He tried to convince me otherwise and kept telling me how much he loved me. I'm thinking to myself like "dude, we just met!" I put all my clothes back on, said my goodbyes and got back to school in time before my mom showed up to pick me up! A few weeks later he got arrested for what I don't even know but I can bet it was probably drug dealing affiliated. He would call my house phone collect and every now and then I would accept it from him.

He would talk about dumb stuff like how he doesn't know how he got caught, or how he was gonna do better once he got out. He was in and out of jail most of our relationship and he would always try to convince me to send him money or put money on his books. I did the one time, but I told him I would not make a habit out of doing this. Honestly, my family and friends knew me well enough to know not to ask me for any money because 9/10, I wasn't giving it up.

A few times he called, and my mother answered the phone. I would get cursed out after she cursed him out first of course! He would then curse me out the next time he called for not picking up the phone before my mama did. I got tired of him really quick because he would always fuss at me as if I was one of his kids; he was only two (2) years older than I.

By the next time he got out I had been working two jobs and I had already bought my first car. He thought he was some kind of pimp or something because he would ask me for money as if he had me out on the streets or something. I had been working one of the jobs the whole summer and I guess feeling generous I would give him money every now and then and hang out while his mom was at work. We would make out, but we never took it any further until this one day, I had made a crazy amount of money that day and with excitement I went over to show him and share my grind fulfillment with him.

He told me how pretty I was, and he was proud of me and started kissing all over my neck. He began taking my clothes off. I told him I was not ready to lose my "virginity" and he told me not to worry, he would "go slow." I most certainly got tired of hearing that from dudes. The next thing I knew he performed sexual acts on me, and I fell asleep ultimately staying the night at his house.

I remember the next morning waking up next to him, and stressing about calling my mom to "check in." He told me to make sure I blocked my number out because my mama definitely knew his last name, which would pop up on the caller ID. I spoke to my mom. She asked me where I was and when I would be coming home because some of my cousins and uncle were visiting. I was excited to see them, so I got my things together, said goodbye to my "boyfriend" and hurried out the apartment.

My plan was to stop at one of the local fast-food restaurants and buy everyone a morning breakfast. I went in my purse to see how much change I had because most of the bills were 50's and 20's and to my surprise I barely had $13 in my purse. I remember counting the money to my "dude" and having $813 CASH from my combined checks from both jobs! At 15 you already know that was a lot of money but like both my parents I was a hustler! (Legally of course.) Now, because I was dealing with a street dude, I had to **assume** he took my money.

I knew I didn't lose it overnight, so I flipped a U-turn and **proceeded** to head back to his apartment. I knocked on the door **frantically**, and he opened it and said, "I knew you would be back!" I thought to myself, "this dude is crazy!" I went in and he told me to wait in his room until he showered and got dressed. But of course, as soon as I heard the water come on, I tried to tear that room apart looking for my money! He came back **suddenly** and sooner than I expected!

"What are you doing?" He asked.

"What do you think I'm doing?" I replied. "I know you stole my money!"

He looked at me with this evil corrupted expression and replied, "You mean my money?"

My jaw literally dropped to the floor. I knew I was NOT going to get my money back without some force! He was a little guy, I thought. "I think I could take him? Ha!" I continued to search through his drawers etc. and he came at me with **rage** and **fury** and slammed me up against the wall! He wrapped his hand around my neck and squeezed like a cobra and said to me, "If you touch my sh__ again, I will kill you!" He let me go, and I ran out of the apartment **hysterical** and with utter **resentment**.

What a fool I looked like, I just laid down with this boy and moments after doing so he robs me! **Agitated,** I drove home with **vengeance** on my mind, and I told my mom and family what happened. My brothers and cousins were ready to pull up! My mom said with the calmest voice I had ever witnessed her using, "Don't get into Sandie's sh___!" Once again, I had to pick my jaw up off the floor!

I was in complete **disbelief**. I just couldn't imagine my family not wanting to support me and aid in my defense. But my mama expressed to me, "I been told you to leave that little trouble making boy alone!" I guess she had a point. But my money though??!! That hurt me to the core. I had worked so hard. And the ninja left me with $13 funky dollars.

My Mama Always Told Me...

Poem

What a fool I've been, I suppose I didn't quite understand.
To give a piece of me away I had been holding on to for so long
Just to be played on command.
I try not to live with regrets, just thinking of it ending as a threat
Gave away my **significant asset**.

The one thing I thought that truly made me special,
Tryna be grown staying out late as if I was some **rebel**.
I should have been more careful; it was like I laid down with the devil.
The choices we make can sometimes haunt us; he wasn't even the one.
I lay that night wanting to cuss and fuss, but I realized that what's done is done.

My mama tried to warn me over and over, but a hard-head girl doesn't listen,
Everything that glitters ain't gold now a piece of me was missin'.
A woman before my time resulting in a crime, man I felt so foolish
He made a believer out of me no doubt it was something completely **senseless**.

Naïve to believe all those times I held him down, got me looking like a straight up clown
I built myself up from the ground just to get knocked right back around.

Think twice, map it out, write out all the pros and cons,
remember you only have one
Then before you know it, it's gone.

If I had it all over to do again, I would have listened to
my mama and avoided all the drama.
As kids we never think our parents know what they know
but it all stems from karma.

If you **reap** what you sow am, I am planting a graveyard
cuz my actions may be observed as deadly,
To be responsible for my behavior yet act as if I didn't
have common sense one would think I was **unsteady**
Demonstrating **mischievousness**.

Vocabulary

1. Mischievousness- able or tending to cause annoyance, trouble, or minor **injury**

2. Senseless- destitute of, deficient in, or contrary to <u>sense</u>

3. Rebel- opposing or taking arms against a government or ruler

4. Significant asset- the entire property of a person, association, corporation, or estate

5. Agitated- troubled in mind: disturbed and upset

6. Vengeance- <u>punishment</u> inflicted in retaliation for an injury or offense

7. Resentment- a feeling of indignant displeasure or persistent ill will at something regarded as a wrong, insult, or injury

8. Hysterical- feeling or showing extreme and unrestrained emotion

9. Fury- extreme fierceness or violence

10. Proceeded- to go on in an orderly regulated way

11. Suddenly- happening or coming unexpectedly

12. Frantically- in a nervously hurried, desperate, or panic-stricken way

13. Naïve- not previously subjected to experimentation or a particular experimental situation

14. Unsteady- not firm or solid: not fixed in position

My Mama Always Told Me...

Something about covering up one eye.

(Lazy eye insecurities HA) 😊

Chapter 20

Sweet and Sexy Sixteen

I don't know what it is about turning 16 working a part time job, driving my own car and not having to rely on anyone but my mama that gave me a sense of **resiliency**. I remember when I got my first pager the week before my 16th birthday. My mama always told me if she paged and I didn't call her back quicker than quick she was gonna tear my behind up.

One day she pages me, I was thinking just to ensure the device was **functional**, but I hurried to call her back and she expressed to me some man came by the house looking for me. My mom was **reactive** to everything I did. Maybe because she had been a parent to three kids before I came along? Sometimes it was **exhausting** having a short leash in her house. She knew I was perfectly **imperfect** though. Nevertheless, I was just happy to know it wasn't the police or anyone crazy looking for me. But we will call him, Suavey.

I knew of this dude only because my friend's brother and he were BFF's. I was curious what he was doing creeping around my house though? My brother was 2 years older than I and this dude was 2 years older than him. Suavey was a flashy kind of dude. Very nice sporty car, money, and lived with his mama and daddy. He was about 21 years old with a full goatee. So, 2/3 wasn't bad in my book. When I returned home, I called him and inquired what it was he needed from me? I quickly learned everything he did was **intentional**. He **expressed** that he heard it was my birthday coming up and he wanted to get me a birthday cake? Strange, I thought. However, ya'll seen the pictures…

I was a big girl and all I could think to myself was, did he say cake? Ha! He came by the day before my birthday to ask what kind of cake I wanted. I have always been a strawberry fan, so my request was a vanilla cake with fresh strawberries on top. He asked what I had planned on doing to my hair and I looked at him as if he was stupid. What was wrong with my hair, I asked him. He expressed to me that it was nothing wrong, but it could always be better.

I guess his mother was a kitchen hairstylist as we used to call them. He offered to have his mama do my hair and he suggested I get a weave sewed in. I grew up with fake ponytails and braids, so my first sew in… Yes please!!! He picked me up and brought me to his house and spoke about how beautiful I was, and I looked better than most of the females his age. (Grown women) So, of course this was flattering, nonetheless. We arrived at his house and he **introduced** me to his mama, and she was a very nice lady I must say.

She asked me a million questions while she styled my hair including my age! I was a little hesitant to let mama dukes know how old I was because if it was my mama, she would have called me a little fast tale girl and shooed me away! However, I expressed to her my age of turning 16 this day and she simply said, "Happy Birthday!" (Insert side eye) She **obviously** didn't seem concerned with her son hanging out with a 16-year-old girl and he was 21.

Eventually it became dark and Ms. Lady was done with my head and ol' boy was ready to take me out he expressed. We went to the movies and he became very touchy feely with me. I sat on the other side of my seat practically and he began scooting closer and closer. His hand crept over to my knee first then sliding up to my thigh. I gently pushed his hand away and still he continued to try and rub and caress my thigh. After **surviving** the movie, he offered to take me to get some ice cream. I was hoping for dinner, but it was already late, and a sweet treat was all he seemed to want to embark on. We sat and briefly chatted about the movie and he continued to admire my "shape" expressing what a "coke bottle shape" I had and to me I felt flattered because I always viewed myself as an overweight kid. Whenever a man or boy complimented or praised me, I would be very **exalted**. Although the older I got, the number I became to the compliments. Especially when I knew there were **hidden agendas** behind the message.

We loaded up in his fancy sports car and drove to the beach in Tacoma. Before we got there, he stopped at the corner store and bought a 6 pack of wine coolers. I expressed to him that I didn't drink, and he assured me that it would taste like juice and I would like it. The night raced by and before I knew it the time was past one a.m. and he had downed 3 drinks and I was still nursing that one. He began kissing my neck and my comfort level went from a 7 to a 3! I told him that I wasn't ready for anything further and he just continued to come closer and closer and finally kissed me lips to lips. He began touching my inner thighs and continued kissing me and he asked me if I was a **virgin**. Now, I knew good and well what that meant however I played it off! I really wasn't interested in doing anything with him. He expressed to me how much he wanted to "taste me." Oral pleasure was my idea of not going all the way (if you know what I mean). But still, I begged him to just drop me off at home.

I knew my mama was gonna curse me out as soon as I got home since by then it was after 2 a.m. He dropped me off at home and stated he would call me later in the day and I secretly hoped he wouldn't! I came in the house filled with smoke, and my mama was nodding off at the kitchen table along with one of her drunk friends and the friends' man. I slowly tipped to my room to avoid the floor creeks. Before I could get all the way to my room my mama looked up, told me Happy birthday, and told me to take my a__ to bed! I was **relieved**! I was really hoping not to get whooped on my birthday. Ol boy called me later that day and told me he wanted to take me out again, but he wanted to get a Hotel room? I knew exactly what that meant! And I was not at all interested. He would continue to call and leave desperate begging voicemails almost daily for over a week or so. I think the fact that he was so much older than myself, I really was not interested in him. Apart of me wondered exactly how dumb did he think I was? It really bothered me that he couldn't find a chick his own age. I remember as a young girl I used to think it was cool when older guys were trying to holler at me but now, I know men like that to **ultimately** be pedophiles!

Poem

Bruh you wild, you wanna sit and act like you ain't know I was a child?
The audacity of him to ask my age, but still result in tryna box me in a cage!
Lose my number my guy, I don't even wanna see you waste my time to try.
These dudes be out here well beyond their years, trying to live without fear.
I don't know what I was thinking taking gifts and playing with imaginary GIF's
The moment I discovered what you were about, I should have ran away with a shout
Do not pass me no drink I'm not of age, I made the choice to **proceed** to center stage
As kids we think that it won't happen to me, like he was really gonna sweep me off my feet
Glad that he wasn't **aggressive** as the others, Boy if I would have went and told my mother
I am quite certain she would have pulled the curtains; he most definitely would have been laid up hurtin
There was one thing about him, he **articulated** himself every chance on a whim
Young girls and older guys, I don't even know why I was surprised.
The fact that his mama had no concern or **conducted** herself while letting my hair burn
Just goes to show she must have been used to this **behavior**; I could tell she was doing him a favor
How many other before me I wondered, I sat up watching the phone ring and pondered.
Found out he had a long-time girlfriend during that time, back then that was hardly a crime.
However, his **credibility** was shot down, he represented every bit of a clown!

Vocabulary

1. **Reactive-** occurring as a result of stress or emotional upset
2. **Resiliency-** an ability to recover from or adjust easily to <u>adversity</u> or change
3. **Exhausting-** to tire extremely or completely
4. **Imperfect-** of, relating to, or constituting a verb tense used to designate a continuing state or an incomplete action especially in the past
5. **Intentional-** done by <u>intention</u> or design
6. **Expressed-** to represent in words to make known the opinions or feelings of (oneself)
7. **Introduced-** to lead to or make known by a formal act, announcement, or recommendation
8. **Obviously-** as is plainly evident
9. **Surviving-** remaining after another or others have ceased existence, operation, or use
10. **Exalted-** elevated in rank, power, or character
11. **Hidden agendas-** an ulterior motive
12. **Virgin-** a person who is inexperienced in a usually specified sphere of activity
13. **Relieved** experiencing or showing <u>relief</u> especially from anxiety or pent-up emotions
14. **Ultimately** in the end : fundamentally eventually -
15. **Proceed-** to come forth from a source to begin and <u>carry on</u> an action, process, or movement
16. **Aggressive-** marked by obtrusive energy and self-assertiveness
17. **Articulated-** expressing oneself <u>readily</u>, clearly, and effectively
18. **Conducted-** to direct or take part in the operation or management of experiment, business, investigation etc.
19. **Behavior-** the way in which someone conducts oneself or behaves
20. **Credibility-** the quality or power of inspiring belief

My Mama Always Told Me…

Chapter 21

Sixteen and Sassy

In order to **value** someone else you must first value yourself. I felt I did things well, however a part of me had a lot of the negative **impactful** things people would say about me growing up and got stuck in my head. I didn't practice a lot of **psychological fitness** if you will. Just a bunch of **character defects** that I began to I let others impact in the **anxiety** I began to develop. When I was young, I experienced an intense amount of childhood **post traumatic stressors**. I exhibited the kind of behavior the young kids now a days would say was that of thirsty **antics**.

I became extremely **depressed**, especially when I would experience **rejection** from members of the opposite sex. Over the course of a few months I would purposefully bury myself in work taking on extra shifts. Even though **child labor law** restricted me working over a certain number of hours as a minor. I didn't care as long as my supervisor didn't mention it to me. I bottled up **trauma** quite often. A bunch of my friends either smoked weed or popped ecstasy pills as leisure passing time.

I became **assertive** about the thought of drugs and being a very well-developed young girl if I wanted something bad enough, I didn't have an issue getting it. I don't think I **comprehended** what suicide was exactly. I mean obviously heard stories of others in my family who had done it and my mom had attempted one time herself that I witnessed at age 7 or 8?

I recall my mom tripping out over dudes and such when they wouldn't do what she wanted and seeing all that blood truly made me **Leery** about going that route. I was never a "cutter" as some of the kids would say. However, I **acquired** the **narcotics** my mama would always tell me to stay out of her sh____! Whenever I would get really down and sad, I would take a handful of pills just to see what would happen?

I never considered if I didn't wake up what impact this would take on my family or if anyone would even care? I was optimistic even when I came to attempt to take my own life. My thoughts would become so cloudy that I would show up to work on days I wasn't scheduled. I would skip class and beat my mom home before that **truancy** phone call came through. I no longer cared about school or work all I cared about was boys.

I started dating this dude who was about 24 years old. He was a scumbag if you asked me. Dingy, grimy, dirtbag with the nastiest teeth and gum disease you would ever see. He stayed with his aunt and uncle. Let him tell it, he was in between homes. I really didn't care; he had a car and would pick me up in the event my car was acting up or not. We hung out for a few months and I quickly began to lose interest in him. I had my little boyfriends on the side, but he was my main dude.

One day I get a phone call that appeared to be urgent. It was him telling me his family's house burnt down and he needed somewhere to stay for a few days. My mom was out of town and I really had little to no adult supervision. I told him he could stay at my house until my mom came back. Boy was I bold to have a whole nig#* staying in my bedroom of my mother's house. One of her men must have called and told her about my **antics** and she called me immediately after.

She fussed, cussed, and yelled for so long I couldn't help but to take the phone away from my ear. I was the boldest little thing you ever did see. Me and my boyfriend were now living together, and I really didn't care if I got caught or not. My brother who at the time was 17 Married with a baby and my mother approved and allowed, so in my mind I didn't see any wrong in what I was doing. My mom returned home and low and behold she busted in my room cupcaking with my lil boyfriend and threw him out so fast he didn't have the opportunity to grab his belongings.

My mama always told me don't pee where you poo… And I honestly just wanted to help this young fella out ultimately. He was the type of guy who didn't have a lot of fans, and basically was thrown to the wolves at a young age and gravitated to the streets in his adolescence. When I first met him, I was not even attracted to him. Back then swag didn't exist, but charisma and finesse did. He was rough around the edges and spoke like a thug, and for some reason I had an increased attraction towards the bad boys.

He was heavily into drugs and often offered to me and I would decline. You gotta wait for the next book to discover what Mama Always told me about Drugs. I didn't share with him any stories of my thoughts of suicide. He brought out a caring representation of me because you see he needed me. And at times I felt he knew I needed him. Age 16 I was 220 pounds and although boys thought I was thick I viewed myself as being Fat.

I wanted boys to like me, but instead I would get men. Isn't that something? I remember girls my age would complain about finding an older dude and the difficulties, but I didn't have that problem. For me, it was totally opposite.

I didn't realize that my little boyfriend had such a complicated drug problem until the one day I came to the hotel a well-known organization sponsored him and his family to stay in temporarily. I opened the door with the extra key he gave me and there he laid on the ground cold and lifeless. I had never seen a dead body before, so I assumed he was playing. I was in shock but went over to shake him and he would not move.

I screamed so loud I swear the windows shook. I began what I saw on television as CPR and beat on his chest. I was fearful I would get blamed for this tragedy and ran to call 911 on the hotel telephone. The staff from the hotel came quickly after being notified of my screams from the next-door guests.

Paramedics were able to **revive** him. Took him to the hospital, and I never saw or heard from him after that. I tried to look him up and could not find anyone remotely close to him. I know that experience taught me more than I thought I needed to know about experimenting with drugs. I developed a savior mentality after that, and boys/men became more of an experiment than anything else.

My Mama Always Told Me...

POEM

"Life is short and then you die" wow that is crazy what they say.
Life has many ups and downs and the balance can be a dismay.
Life has many unexpected twists and turns to duck and dodge every day.
Life can shake raddle and roll leaving impressions out to play.
Life can catch you by surprise if you veer off and stray.
Life has the implications to shape and mold you nothing short of **crochet**.
Life will teach you vital lessons and only meet you halfway.
Life doesn't care if you are struggling mentally or stuck in the driveway.
Life may not be what you want it to be but there will be an open doorway.
Life will struggle and teach you each moment has its purpose & gateway.
Life can't help but make its presence known whether you want it to delay.
Life is love and leisure even if you really do hate to hit replay.
Life is all in what you make it, make each day nothing short of some great reggae.
Life is unforeseen don't travel down the wrong roadway
Life will make you listen and learn like football play by play.
Life doesn't care if you're a boy or a girl it will take hold of your airway.
Life may flicker and flutter your heart put you down like

a cigarrete in an ashtray.
Life is beautiful, alluring, marvelous nothing short like a dance at a ballet.
Life may be tarnished, uncertain, even dark some days may be cloudy and gray.
But Life is everything comforting, hopeful and exciting if you sing like a blue jay

Vocabulary

1. **Crochet-** needlework consisting of the interlocking of looped stitches formed with a single thread and a hooked needle
2. **Value-** relative worth, utility, or importance
3. **Impactful-** having a forceful impact : producing a marked impression
4. **Psychological Fitness-** directed toward the will or toward the mind specifically in its conative function-- the condition of being sound in body

5. **Character Defects-** conduct that conforms to an accepted standard of right and wrong -- something that spoils the appearance or completeness of a thing
6. **Anxiety-** an uneasy state of mind usually over the possibility of an anticipated misfortune or trouble
7. **Post Traumatic Stressors-** A disorder in which a person has difficulty recovering after experiencing or witnessing a terrifying event.
8. **Antics-** a playful or mischievous act intended as a joke
9. **Depressed-** feeling unhappiness-- kept from having the necessities of life or a healthful environment
10. **Child Labor Law-** Child labor laws are statutes placing restrictions and regulations on the work of minors
11. **Trauma -** a disordered psychic or behavioral state resulting from severe mental or emotional stress or physical injury
12. **Assertive-** disposed to or characterized by bold or confident statements and behavior
13. **Comprehended-** to grasp the nature, significance, or meaning of understanding
14. **Leery-** feeling or showing a lack of trust in someone or something

15. **Acquired-** attained as a new or added characteristic, trait, or ability
16. **Narcotics-** a drug (such as marijuana or LSD) subject to restriction similar to that of addictive narcotics whether physiologically
17. **Optimistic-** feeling or showing hope for the future
18. **Truancy-** an act or instance of playing truant
19. **Antics-** an attention-drawing, often wildly playful or funny act or action
20. **Revive-** to return to consciousness or life: become active or flourishing again

Chapter 22

My best friends' drunken brother

I grew up where not only did I have my mama telling me to stop being a little fast tailed girl, but my sister **spewed** this logic as well. I developed a **complex** where if anyone's man or male family member was around I would "Stay in my place." My best friend had this older brother. He was probably a good 6 years older than me. When I was 17 you couldn't tell me, I wasn't "grown." I was working, drove my own car, and paid my own cellular phone bill. Ha! Oh, to be young again.

I would go over my friends' house almost every day after school. My mama always told me when she had company to get lost if you will. So, when I wasn't at work (which I used to feel like I was there often,) I would go hang out at my friends. We would sit up and do each other's hair or watch music videos or just talk. Her older brother would come into her room and fall on the bed next to me and say all kind of goofy stuff. I guess he thought he was mackin, but I really wasn't checking for him. I already had about 2 dudes on the team, and to add another would just be too **complicated**.

We often locked him out the room to have our private time and chill. But when he figured out how to **jimmy the lock** when he was home, we ran out of ways to keep him out. I could tell he wanted attention and probably needed someone to talk to. On days my friend had to work, I would go over her house anyway just to pretend I wanted to see her, but I really grew a liking towards him and felt bad for him.

He was in and out of jail and based off the **reputation** I heard about him he really wasn't all that popular. Ran with the local gang and smoked and drank as did most of the dudes I was interested in at that time. What is it about a bad boy that drew me to their **demeanor** I thought? I always wanted to **extricate** these guys that were unmotivated to do well in life. They were **disengaged** and sexually **liberated** in my opinion. Seems like all they wanted to do was get high, have sex and play video games. This was most of the dudes I knew, and the others were gang banging and running the streets robbing folks.

I had a great deal of **empathy** for the men in my life. I shared their pain and sorrow, and **unbeknownst** to me the reaction would be **invigorating** to them. Finally, someone (A woman) who cared or acknowledged what it was they were feeling. I believe I learned this from my mama. She was the who's who when it came to the men, and her relationship with women was catty. The fellas would gravitate towards her welcoming, energetic, responsive **aura**.

One night I went to my friend's house and she was at getting ready for work on this evening. Her brother appeared to be intoxicated sitting on the couch watching a basketball game. I passed by the living room and his eyes connected with mine. I knew what that look represented, as I had seen it time and time again from others. I went to use the restroom and before I could come out the door, he pounced on me like a cheetah on a gazelle!

He began touching and rubbing my breast and booty. Grabbing me to come closer and closer to him. And asked if he could kiss me. I nudged him away thinking he was just playing but I caught a sense of rejection when this took place. He was very adamite about a kiss and I really just didn't want to do that to my friend. I could imagine the **disappointment** she would feel if she knew I slept with or even kissed her brother. His grip was that of the Kungfu and I could not fight him off hard enough without causing pain or **discomfort** to him. I wanted to claw his face like a dagblasted irritable itch, but I feared what he would do to me if I did.

After **squirming** and pushing he finally released me and asked what my problem was? The nerve I thought, but then I realized he was far from sober and although he may have been attractive to me, he had never behaved like this before. My mama always told me "a drunk mind speaks a sober heart." So, I knew he wanted me in that way, but I just didn't see this happening. He stormed off and slammed his room door. My friend heard the slam (as did the rest of the house) and she came running towards the bathroom.

What is going on? She **expressed** to me. I don't even know I replied with an uncertain lie. She went to go check on him and he refused to open the door. She banged and banged but the knocks went unanswered. He really must be loaded she **exclaimed**. Was he out here with you? She asked. Not really, he was on the couch getting drunk, I expressed. I believe he was on the phone with someone who may have upset him? Boy, my mama always told me I would make a good lawyer because lying I did well!

A few days went by and I stayed away from my friend's house to avoid her brother. She invited me over to their family dinner one Sunday evening and although leery I agreed to attend. Her brother was sitting at the other end of the table, and he kept **gleaming** a hole like a laser gun through my head. I wanted to say something but didn't want to make anyone uncomfortable. He got up from the table once he finished his food and came over to me and whispered in my ear. "Meet me in the back yard." My friend had a real dope patio out back of her house and a swing set I believe her father built the year before he passed away. The brother asked me if I could forgive him for the other night. Said he was hella drunk and would never try to hurt or harm me. Said he really valued our friendship and although his sister was my friend, he looked at me like I was his friend as well. I thanked him for his apology and told him it was all good.

 Don't let it happen again I joked but was serious. He expressed it wouldn't but told me that he really did like me. I told him it was ok to like me, but I didn't want to upset his sister by taking our friendship any further.

We are still very good friends today, and he always brings up that night and what could have happened. I know that deep down he didn't mean to push up on me in that way, but also realize that he had never behaved like that towards me before. He was a good dude, just had some hang ups that I am proud to say he has resolved in his adulthood.

Poem

A true friend indeed no one could say I wasn't. The respect I possessed was that like none other. No one could compare the representation I had for them that was. I wanted to be that and more that I desired for someone to be for me. I would sacrifice it all just to be that leader in peaceful serene. The way I carried myself was that of a gem indeed. I had to show them what they were missing out on and make it clear as a bright sunny day. I respected others more than myself and for that I am greatly disappointed at times I would sit and lay. I would do for them at any given rhyme. I wanted to protect the identity of those who hurt and harmed me, but who was protecting me. I fell short on the self-love tip and created toxic memories. The reach of those who came my way left boundaries unmet. My mindset changed when I saw how others did what I couldn't, and the rain fell on those days when I wondered who would do the same that I wouldn't? Whether a brother or friend or uncle or son the dynamics never changed. I thought of how I could make things better. My heart was heavy for those hurting and my mind would wander with thoughts of how I could help or be of service. I continued this path for years to come never wanting to be a burden. But the burden would have been better than harboring the ill feelings and thoughts of those I encountered.

Vocabulary

1. **Spewed-** material that exudes or is extruded
2. **Complex-** hard to separate, analyze, or solve
3. **Jimmy the lock-** is to force it open
4. **Reputation-** recognition by other people of some characteristic or ability
5. **Extricate-** to free or remove from an entanglement or difficulty
6. **Demeanor-** behavior toward others : outward manner
7. **Disengaged-** emotionally detached
8. **Liberated-** freed from or opposed to traditional social and sexual attitudes or roles
9. **Empathy-** the action of understanding, being aware of, being sensitive to, and vicariously experiencing the feelings, thoughts, and experience of another of either the past or present without having the feelings, thoughts, and experience fully communicated in an objectively explicit manner
10. **Unbeknownst-** happening or existing without the knowledge of someone specified
11. **Invigorating-** having an enlivening or stimulating effect
12. **Aura-** a subtle sensory stimulus (such as an aroma)
13. **Squirming-** to twist about like a worm : fidget
14. **Gleaming-** a transient appearance of subdued or partly obscured light

My Mama Always Told Me...

Chapter 23

My homegirls man

Growing up being called a little fast tale little girl if I did so much as smiled or looked at a boy or man. The older I got the more **assertive** I became around men, but someone else's man? That was created a **discontent mentality** in me. Sometimes my behavior was **relentless,** but I would **resent** the decisions I made.

I had this friend who juggled multiple dudes like it was a **habitual** characteristic. She had a main one who would always greet me with an intense **embrace** that made me every bit of uncomfortable. His strong cologne would linger and **resonate** for quite some time after the interaction. Whenever they would invite me and my dude over, he would make it a point to comment how "thick" I was getting. (I felt I looked fat, but that's neither here nor there). His apartment was very nice and clean especially for a man. However, I knew my friend probably helped keep things in order and such.

My friend told me what a major D-boy her dude was. (Dope dealer) She complained about their intimate **interactions**, but she stayed because he bought her any and everything she wanted. She would always **boast** how much money he would have her count for him. I didn't really want to know what illegal activities they had going on because being an **accomplice** was not on my list of things to do. One day she called me from a major department store and asked me what size I wore because he she wanted to grab me a few things while he was **splurging** anyway. **Embarrassed** to share my size, I merely gave her my dress size (smaller than my pant size) and welcomed the free designer clothing.

It became routine that we would all get together every other Saturday night and either play cards or a silly board game. They all would partake in smoking festivities and I would either sit and watch with my shirt or jacket covering my face. Or I would go in the bedroom and wait until the coast was clear. On this one storming rainy Saturday evening, I decided to go in the bedroom and chill on the recliner chair positioned in the corner of the room. Within 5 minutes of the living room filling with smoke the dude came peeking in the bedroom. He sat close to me in a stool that was used as decoration. He inquired as to why I never would **partake** in the smoke **hoopla**. I shared with him a time when I was about 12 and had smoked with a close friend and had a dang **panic attack** and fell down the hallway flight of stairs. Epic Fail if I don't say so myself.

He offered to "take good care of me" if anything similar was to happen. He skootched closer and closer to me taking his hand and stroking up and down my arm. I declined the offer and stated that it just wasn't for me. He tried to persuade me over the next 6-8 minutes getting even closer and dang near sitting in the recliner chair next to me although it was clearly made for one body and not two. He was **interrupted** by my dude bursting in the door. "What the heck are you doing Sandie" he fussed. I swear it reminded me of my mama yelling. Nothing, I fussed back. Let's go he said. And I quickly jumped up, apologized to my friend while being escorted out of the door by my dude.

"What the heck was that all about?" He **investigated**. I didn't do anything, I quickly replied. "It didn't look like nothing!" He yelled. Stop yelling at me! I fussed. He lowered his voice and asked the same question. "What was that all about", he spoke in a low tone and calm tempered voice. My boyfriend was in his early 20's so he demonstrated a more mature demeanor than the boys I had dated that were closer in my age. He wanted me to come smoke with you all, I expressed. "Why!?" he fussed. Afraid and **intimidated**, I expressed I don't even know. He got quiet the rest of the car ride to my house and stated, "don't be letting no dudes try to get at you!" before he let me out of his car. "I'm gonna check his as_ next time I see him," he fussed. Ok, I said with fear and hesitation.

As soon as I got in the house I ran to my room and quickly called my friend. I told everything that happened, and she brushed it off like she always did with me. She responded saying "he probably just wanted to see how goofy you get when you are high!" How would he know if I get goofy? I asked her. She admitted to telling him about the story I had also told her earlier in the night. Embarrassed, I asked why she would tell him this. She expressed he would always wonder why I didn't partake in the smoke sessions with them. You could have told him I was allergic or something!!! I yelled at her. She hung up in my face. Irritated, I called back repeatedly, and she wouldn't pick up. I was trying to blow her dang phone up!

Ashamed, I called his phone and asked to speak to her? I had his number saved from the time she called me from his house phone because in one of their heated arguments he broke her phone and she had no other way to contact me. He expressed that she had packed all her stuff and left. "What did you say to her?" He expressed. "I told her the truth," I said irritated and embarrassed. "Why did you do that?" He **inquired**. Because I can! I snapped. "Hmph" he replied. "You want me to pick you up so we can go find her" he said.

We really had no business hanging out with this old dude in the first place. We were both only 16 years old and this guy had to be in his mid-30's. My friend stayed with this guy for almost a year, continuing to get abused and tormented. We stopped contacting each other because she was obviously embarrassed, and I just didn't want to hear any more about this loser she decided to deal with.

I never brought him up again, mainly because she ran through so many dudes I don't even know if it fazed her or not. I guess you could say, I looked up to her in a lot of ways. My Mama Always Told Me, that if I wanted to end up just like her, I better go live with her and her mama. My mother didn't like her, but she also was not her biggest fan due to her lies and deceitful behavior. But she was my main friend for so many years I just didn't know how to leave her be. Sometimes it's difficult to part ways with a **toxic** friend. But it is very necessary.

Poem

A friend is a person to tell all your secrets,
but keeping the bad ones can hurt in a sense.
A friend is a person you can depend on and lean on,
but when things go wrong it makes the relationship tense.
A friend is a person you should hold to a high standard,
but when they fall short just know they will leave their presence.
A friend is a person you can rely on for good advice,
but when they do the total opposite don't get on defense.
A friend is a person that you can laugh and tell jokes with,
but when the arguments come anticipate great suspense.
A friend is a person you want to share exciting moments,
but when they don't listen try not to impart self-defense.
A friend is a person you wanna go out to shop with,
but when you're the only one coming out the pockets for all the expense.
A friend is a person you hoped to share great moments,
but when they don't share back consider things can get dense.
A friend is a person that enjoys being together,
but when they give their time to a lover you can't expect it to not get intense.
A friend is a person you love and loves you back,
but when the love diminishes you must learn to be strong and give your two cents.

Vocabulary

1. **Assertive-** <u>disposed</u> to or characterized by bold or confident statements and behavior
2. **Discontent mentality-** lack of satisfaction with one's possessions, status, or situation: lack of contentment
3. **Relentless-** showing or promising no abatement of severity, intensity, strength, or pace
4. **Resent-** to feel or express annoyance or <u>ill will</u>
5. **Habitual-** regularly or repeatedly doing or practicing something or acting in some manner
6. **Embrace-** to clasp in the arms : hug
7. **Resonate-** to relate harmoniously: strike a chord
8. **Interactions-** mutual or reciprocal action or influence
9. **Boast-** a cause for pride-- a statement expressing excessive pride in oneself
10. **Accomplice-** one associated with another especially in wrongdoing
11. **Splurging-** an ostentatious effort, display, or expenditure
12. **Embarrassed-** feeling or showing a state of self-conscious confusion and distress
13. **Hoopla-** excitement surrounding an event or situation, especially when considered to be unnecessary fuss
14. **Partake-** to take part in or experience something along with others

15. **Panic attack-** a sudden feeling or episode of panic
a brief episode of intense fear or dread that is of sudden onset and typically subsides within 30 minutes, usually occurs for no apparent reason but may sometimes be associated with an identifiable triggering stimulus (such as an existing phobia), and is accompanied by a sense of unreality and impending loss of control and by various debilitating physical symptoms (such as increased heart rate, chest pain, dizziness, and shortness of breath)
16. **Investigated-** to observe or study by close examination and systematic inquiry
17. **Intimidated-** made to feel timid : affected or held back by feelings of fear or timidity

Chapter 24

"Your too old playa"

I was working a few jobs the summer I turned 17. The amusement park a few cities away was probably one of my favorite jobs as an adolescent. Not only did I get to spend countless hours surrounded by kids and young adults, I made some pretty good money as well. I enjoyed **meditating** when I was alone and **exploring** the park on my break. As employees, we got to take advantage of some pretty good deals. Free **admission** on our days off, **discounted** food, and so much more. At this point, I was a **maniac** when it came to **attractive** boys! I guess you could say my mama always told me I was a fast tale little girl.

So now, working my own job I scouted them out every chance I could get! While driving my own vehicle, I would think about the one I see the day before. Knowing I was making money I really didn't have to share with anyone else. (Every blue moon mama would ask to hold a little something) But really, I thought I was grown! It didn't really **resonate** with me that not all boys were good for me. I really **evolved** over the years to think that I could have any guy I wanted. The issue was, they all wanted me in a different way than I wanted them. (Sexually) ☹

I **embraced** members of the opposite sex. Even at a young age, I **recognized** when I could get a guy to do whatever I wanted him to do. The **influences** at the time in my life dating multiple different guys at a time, they were like science projects or a code I needed to crack! On this **particular** day, this dude I scoped working at the amusement park was chocolate like I liked them. (I got that from my mama). His style was quite **impressive**, and his swag was on 10. Okay maybe 8 but I could work with an 8. ☺ I was afraid to **approach** him for some reason though. I could tell he was older than I. He had to be at least 21 or 22? But as a young girl the thrill of dating an older guy or having one on your "team" was like an **accomplishment**. I never realized until I became an adult that we call those kinds of folks' **pedophiles**.

At the time, one of my exes was working at the same park I did. We **developed** a great friendship after we broke up and got over each other I guess you could say? Friendly enough to slide a note I wrote to the handsome dude I discovered at work that day. Me and my good friendly ex went on lunch together and he gassed me up you could say to try and holler at the dude. I wrote him a popular Musiq soulchild lyric "I'm not trying to pressure you, just can't stop thinking about you. You ain't even really gotta be my "boyfriend" (I wrote). Ending the note with my phone number and of course the **infamous** smiley face! His response was passive, and he practically curved me. I was never the type to sweat no dude for the simple fact, I was usually the one being hunted like an antelope in the safari.

A few weeks went by and I looked for him every day I went to work just so I could be "seen." I managed to get a text from him after work one day asking if I wanted to kick it for the 4th of July. He lived with his mother and little brother which made alone time near impossible. He asked if I wanted to ride around to find somewhere to watch the fireworks? (I know what he really wanted to do!) I agreed and since he didn't have a car, I ended up picking him up and we drove around for about an hour. As a teenager I was very cognitive about my gas, and at this point he had not gotten paid yet just like myself. We pulled up into the park and after making out for a good ten minutes, he began to remove my shirt.

Next thing I knew, we were doing adult things in my car in the park. Ugh, I felt so ratchet and worthless afterwards. We didn't even know each other that well. We spoke a few times after and a couple weeks later he stopped returning my phone calls and text. A few months went by and he hit me up saying he lost his phone and my number. The season for the water park was over and I couldn't look for him at work anymore, not that I really wanted to after that night. He would call me just for sex, not to hang out or spend time together. Just sex. I would oblige every now and then in hopes to get closer to him.

But he really didn't want a girlfriend, he just wanted to "hit" and that was it. I would question if he had a girl and maybe was just not telling me and he would deny. I met his little brother by accident one day leaving his house and he was trying to slip me his number on the low. Why do guys do this? Like the old saying goes, "It ain't fun if the homies can't have none" **mentality**? I just wasn't that type of girl. I didn't mess with homeboys. Well, there was that one time, but you will have to check that out the next book.

This guy was definitely not what my mama told me about when it came to men. She really never even met him, mainly because he was just not that important to me. Yet, I was sharing my body with him. We continued on and off for a few years I guess you could say he was my "hump buddy." We rarely used **protection**, and I am quite certain he burnt me multiple times. (Burnt is the term used for spreading a sexually transmitted disease) Eventually he ended up getting me pregnant. And that is what ended our relationship (if that's what you want to call it) I never really got to know him until years later which we will discuss book #2 going into My Mama Always Told… Baby girl Keep Your Legs Closed.

POEM

A young girl was she just wanted to be seen,
Not the wisest decisions you would agree,
chasing boys all in these streets.
They said, "the darker the berry the sweeter the juice,"
Guess that's what turned me on to you.
Charismatic full of fun, look at how you had me good and done.
Do guys mature fully at a certain age?
I hoped to attain your interest like a good book turning each page.
Wanting to be seen, wanting to be loved.
Dumb mistakes of not putting on a love glove.
Some Men will pervert a young girl just assuming, youthful life not intending to ruin. Juggling guys left and right, behold when those feelings catch flight.
You were nothing more than a fling, hardly anticipated a diamond ring.
I did love the way you would sing.
Sad unguided young man you were, your mother shamed your father made you feel like you were sometimes not a bother.
A misguided spirit was he, no direction no determination for great things.
Just living each day like life didn't even matter,
chasing after butts that would only make you sadder.
Heart getting broke time and time again, a sensitive man that could hardly even stand.
Abusing drugs and women as if some sort of sport, how was I to know you desired some **cohort**.
Wanted to be a friend without benefits if you cared, but low and behold that was not of interest to you I should have made myself aware.

My Mama Always Told Me...

Vocabulary

1. **Meditating-** to engage in <u>contemplation</u> or reflection
2. **Exploring-** to investigate, study, or analyze look into
3. **Admission-** an act of <u>admitting</u> : the fact or state of being admitted
4. **Discounted-** a reduction made from the gross
5. **Resonate-** to produce or exhibit <u>resonance</u>- to relate harmoniously : strike a chord message that *resonates* with voters
6. **Maniac-** a person characterized by an inordinate or ungovernable enthusiasm for something
7. **Attractive-** arousing interest or pleasure : CHARMING
8. **Evolved-** to produce by natural <u>evolutionary</u> processes
9. **Embraced-** to take in or include as a part, item, or element of a more inclusive whole
10. **Recognized-** to acknowledge or take notice of in some definite way
11. **Influences-** the power or capacity of causing an effect in indirect or intangible ways
12. **Impressive-** making or tending to make a marked <u>impression</u> : having the power to excite attention, awe, or admiration
13. **Accomplishment-** the act or fact of <u>accomplishing</u> something : completion
14. **Pedophiles-** sexual <u>perversion</u> in which children are the preferred sexual object

15. **Developed-** having a relatively high level of industrialization and standard of living
16. **Infamous-** having a reputation of the worst kind
17. **Protection-** the act of <u>protecting</u> : the state of being <u>protected</u>
18. **Mentality-** <u>mental</u> power or capacity : intelligence
19. **Abusing-** a corrupt practice or custom-- improper or excessive use or treatment
20. **Cohort-** a group of individuals having a statistical factor (such as age or class membership) in common in a demographic study

Chapter 25

Boys need protection too

This has got to be the most difficult chapter of this book for me, because my children mean more to me than they will ever know! I pray that no one must ever experience this hurt and pain, and my transparency in this chapter I hope will help someone someday.

To anyone who suspects their child has been taken advantage of in a sexual or violent manner... I beg you to seek help immediately! Don't wait or be afraid to come forth with any information or even a hunch when it comes to our children, we are their main advocate!

At age 19 I had my first child. The biological father was nothing short of **unprepared** to have a child! He was very **immature** and all the way up until the **paternity test** came back, he denied my child but had never denied hooking up before that! He told me because he smoked a lot of trees, he was incapable of having any babies. Whoever told him that was completely wrong!

Even after the paternity test came back, he wanted nothing to do with my child. He would hang up on me when I would call, and he even convinced his mama that I was some tramp who tried to trap him. I soon **realized** that I had to be a mama and a daddy to my baby boy.

My boyfriend at the time stepped up though and helped out **tremendously** with my handsome young boy whom I nursed over a year to ensure his intelligence was on point! I read in a book that breastfeeding helps babies' brains grow strong and **immensely** smart little kiddos.

He grew to be a very savvy, **intuitive** young man. He excelled in math and although late to speak and read, once he started, he could not stop! After a few short years I felt as if he needed a sibling to come along and embark on life's journey with him. At age five my big man became a Big Brother. The church we attended had a plethora of women and girls I felt I could trust and since I **assumed** everyone who attended church were good, honest and trustworthy people I didn't see any harm in asking sister so-and-so to keep my son upon going into **labor**.

Sister so-and-so worked in the day care at the church we attended, and I made **arrangements** with her to keep my child while I was in the hospital for a few days, a total of two days. I remember when my oldest son came back home with me and his **demeanor** and **disposition** seemed peculiar to say the least. The presence of my child was completely disengaged and **ultimately,** I could

observe a drastic change in his behavior.

I began to question him about the noticeable transformation and a few weeks after I had given birth the gal Sister So-and-So began acting really funny styled, if you will. I remember inviting her and her family to my son's birthday party and she expressed to me that all I wanted was gifts from them for my son.

I thought to myself, Self "Is it not normal to celebrate a child's birthday?

Self, "is celebrating a child turning another year older not something people **typically** do with their children?

The behavior of this girl began to get more and more suspicious. She would kick him out of children's church every week reporting that his conduct was unacceptable, and he would not be **permitted** to play with other children. I began to dig a little deeper with her and her response was dreadfully defensive. She began speaking to me as if I had not known her for years, like I was just some chick off the streets! I retaliated very immaturely, stooping to her level and for weeks we went back-and-forth about my child.

But I honestly didn't feel it was that serious to **vigor** with her because she felt my son didn't belong in the church daycare with all the other children playing and having a good time. He practically grew up in this church and everyone that I knew closely watched him or took care of him at some point in time. As the old saying goes "it takes a village" was **immensely** on my mind since there was an issue with him, plus I wasn't the only one taking care of him. At that time my son was too young to **articulate** what happened to him so all he could say when I asked him what was going on with him, he expressed "she told me to put her thing in my mouth". Instantly I began to cry!

My eyes filled with a mixture of tears and **rage**. I interrogated him multiple times to ensure his story did not change. He expressed to me that before his brother came, Sister So-and-So would force him to suck her breast. He gave me the most awful, **appalling,** and disgusting details about her touching his private parts as we call them and rubbing his penis.

I thought what an **atrocious** monster to take advantage of a young boy and rob him of his innocence. I hugged my little boy so tight, called non-emergency soon after discovering the story and filed a report with the police department against Sister So-and-So. I had my son begin therapy sessions to ensure that "hurt people don't hurt people!"

I wished that I had noticed the red flags sooner because after filing the report I was told that the **statute** of **limitations** had passed of the timeframe that I would have had to report this to the authorities. I wish I had protected him better. I wish I had taken my son to the hospital with me, if **permitted** and I wished he never had to experience such a **barbarian** who would completely take advantage of a young innocent boy.
Just remember boys need protection too.

My Mama Always Told Me...

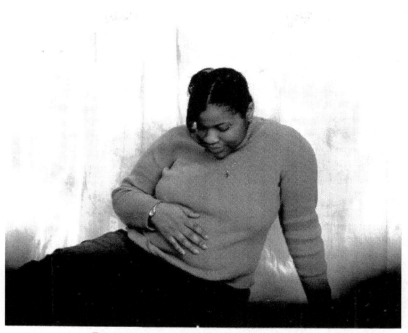

Pregnant at age 18, Delivered at age 19.
(Isaiah Emmanuel Ailep) Now Johnson

Poem

He's only a little boy I thought.

Back in the day, most knew I was not one to shout and fight
But this right here hit home and I can only imagine him feeling alone
A trusted "friend" gave her word to me
To look after my little boy, that was my baby
It's a wonder I didn't go crazy, I tried to find her. I rode around, mind hazy

Then to pick a fight as if she knew I knew what a wicked heart
All along in the dark, as he played in the park conversations would start
As I tried to embark
Saw reflections of a time he had no fear, as my eyes began to shove out a sea full of tears
Women predators are out there you see, I would've never thought it could happen to me

I was in a vulnerable predicament and she took advantage she did
Years went by and she kept that mess hid
Deviant chick completely sick in the head
Worse nightmare fearing for our children trying to keep them out of Harm's way
If I ever see her again, she better hope I turn away to pray.

Vocabulary

1. **Unprepared-** not prepared
2. **Immature-** exhibiting less than an expected degree of maturity
3. **Paternity test-** a test especially of DNA or genetic traits to determine whether a given man could be the biological father of a given child
4. **Realized-** to bring into concrete existence : ACCOMPLISH
5. **Tremendously-** to a great or tremendous extent : EXTREMELY
6. **Immensely-** to a very great or immense degree or extent : exceedingly, enormously
7. **Intuitive-** possessing or given to intuition or insight
8. **Assumed-** not true or real: deliberately pretended or feigned
9. **Arrangements-** the state of being arranged : order-- something made by arranging parts or things together
10. **Labor-** expenditure of physical or mental effort especially when difficult or compulsory
11. **Demeanor-** behavior toward others : outward manner
12. **Disposition-** the act or the power of disposing or the state of being disposed
13. **Ultimately-** in the end : fundamentally-- eventually
14. **Observe-** to inspect or take note of as an augury, omen, or presage
15. **Permitted-** to consent to expressly or formally
16. **Vigor-** active bodily or mental strength or force
17. **Immensely-** to a very great or immense degree or extent : exceedingly, enormously

18. **Articulate-** expressing oneself readily, clearly, and effectively
19. **Rage-** violent and uncontrolled anger
20. **Appalling-** inspiring horror, dismay, or disgust
21. **Atrocious-** appalling, horrifying-- utterly revolting : abominable
22. **Therapy-** treatment intended to relieve or heal a disorder.
23. **Statute-** an international instrument setting up an agency and regulating its scope or authority
24. **Limitations-** an act or instance of limiting-- the quality or state of being limited
25. **Permitted-** to consent to expressly or formally-- to make possible
26. **Barbarian-** uncivilized, or violent —used chiefly in historical references

My Mama Always Told Me…

Isaiah and I on the waterfront beach in Tacoma.

(3 months old)

Isaiah and I took pictures practically every month!

(4 months old)

Enjoying a fun day at the beach! (He loved oranges!)

My Mama Always Told Me...

Me and my mama poem

My mama always told me sticks and stones can break your bones, but words will never hurt you...
I soon discovered the words that came out of her mouth had grenades and rocket launchers.

My entire elementary experience as far as I could remember was filled with yells and curse words every morning before school.
I remember my teacher asking me if I was OK, like she could read the hurt on my face

But as I grinned and shrugged my shoulders, I continued to stay quiet and play
My mama would pick me up after school and ask me "how was your day?"

I figured maybe she forgot how it started top of the morning, so I'd reply it was OK
She'd make me a snack when we got home and tell me to go outside and stay

I'd come back hours later tired but hungry hoping dinner would be on the way
My mama always cooked up something scrumptious, my favorite thanksgiving turkey with a little gray-vay

But mama had issues I never knew would always get in the way,
A bond I hoped to build, grow closer, don't push me away.

A girl's dream is to be just like her mama, in every single way
I remember before my mom ever ate, she would take a few moments to pray over her plate.

Growing up catholic she'd do that up then down cross left then cross right thing with her hand then kiss her finger
But we went to Christian Churches on some Sundays mama had to turn down her ringer.

Middle school got a little better, but I still remember wetting the bed
Traumatized Lil girl, couldn't get that mess outta my head

Mama stop doing my hair she said girl you old enough to do it yourself
I struggled in the mornings and although she knew I needed her, she wouldn't offer me any help

Thank goodness I made some Lil friends, they introduced me to a weave I dealt with them long term
My hair was short and unmanageable them dang just for me perms

My mama challenged who I was becoming without her, no longer relying on her help
I graduated from grenades and rocket launchers to Missiles and Ar15s stealth

High school was tough since she didn't keep up whether I was going to school or not
She ain't even know that's when I really started to act like I wanted to be a Lil thot

Catching rides with young men and grown boys a dangerous life to live
Rebellious to the rules of a single mama but what did I know I grew up in a world full of sin

Seeking my mama's attention, striving to be that intelligent young lady I hoped she was rooting for
Not realizing the moment would pass and she waited til I moved out and shut behind me the door

Motivational song

Keep Your head up!

Keep your head up, have no
worries keep your head up girl
God's going to make a way
Keep your head up, no worries, keep your head up girl!
Don't keep stressing claim your blessings no
worries keep your head up girl
Keep your head up no worries keep your head up girl

I know that things get hard, your life seems somewhat
rough
But girl put down your guard, continue show
me your tough
It's just a matter of time that things get better for you, I
know you'll do just fine
God's going to see you through!

We thank God for your love, and we thank God
for your grace
And we thank you for your mercy that fulfills this holy
place
We thank God for your love, and we thank God
for your grace
And we thank you for your mercy that fulfills this holy
place

Stressing won't prove your point come on and stand on
his word
Turn up on Satan

Stressing won't prove your point
Just stand on his word! Turn up on Satan!

Keep your head up no worries keep your head up girl
God's gonna make a way
Keep your head up, no worries keep your head up girl
Don't keep stressing claim your blessing
No worries keep your head up girl!

(This is the first song I wrote in celebration of the girls I mentor in my program.)

Keep your head up (**The Remix**)

People are going to tell you hatefully that you can't do it but girl you'll get through!
Family's going to wish you failure friend's will
doubt Your potential cuz they're counterfeit
Don't even worry it'll get better

Keep your head up, keep your head up
Keep your head up, keep your head up
Keep your head up, keep your head up (**Keep repeating this to yourself!**)

Remember God shaped every part of you
He knew this day would come through
To see you manage boo boo
Make a believer out of all of them
Get you a whole new crew
Show them how you do!

Remember that you're SAUCY!
Come on girl and stay FLOSSY!
Girl you can keep it BOSSY!
And shine cuz you're Glossy!

Clap back at the haters strategically
Prepare your mind, stay doing so continuously
Show the naysayers this was no accident
This was no mistake no science experiment
Progress and purpose will build you spiritually
Growth and development flow so Heavenly
Remember your purpose this is your specialty
Flow through the room as if you did it so cleverly!

(I wrote this song to help encourage the girls I mentor next! Gotta have a REMIX)

My Mama Always Told Me...

Epilogue

I'm coming to you from a damaged yet healing place. I am no victim. I am no sufferer. I am no pushover. I am a **fearless, strong, intelligent Black Woman**! I have overcome a great deal of hardships. (Just as an adolescent). This is barely scratching the surface. But as an innocent, loving and caring young girl I made some bad choices. Because everything my mama told me went in one ear and out the other, the hardship I struggled through was a result of those bad choices. Some that I just couldn't avoid, some I didn't know during the moments, and some I was very knowledgeable of what I was doing but I didn't quite know why I conducted myself this way.

I had a bold, confident, and courageous personality, and my mama didn't quite know what to do with me. Sometimes my daring demeanor would come off as "fast" as the seasoned generation would say, but I just wanted to be heroic. I wanted to take chances and I wanted to see what my outcome would be regardless of the circumstances from home. But when home got to be unsafe, at times I didn't know who to turn to or flat out turn to anyone who was willing to acknowledge me.

To conclude (**for now**) I went about some things the wrong way and I struggled, and I thought I learned valuable lessons but unfortunately the lessons continued to happen. Reflecting on these stories allowed me to do better going forward. After 18 I continued to bump my head again and again. And I thought, of course I did! No one was sitting me down telling me why I should

avoid these types of situations because no one knew what I had experienced. Now, I know how to manage my curious behavior in the presence of the fellas, and my relationships with women is getting much better.
I remember a lady once told me she didn't "trust women who didn't have other women friends" and unknowingly she was sitting right next to one. I wanted to desperately seek the guidance from other women, but I was afraid to ask for help.

Ultimately, I was looking for love in any and every place and this behavior became "normal" at one time.
But that's another story you will have to be on the "lookout" for.
I merely want to encourage teenage girls, women with daughters, father's with daughters and care providers to take heed to the behaviors and actions of young girls. Some of the signs are right there in your face and if you love and care for the wellbeing of your little ones you will seek professional help for guidance and direction. Most certainly don't ever forget about our young boys! They need protection as well.

In 2017 I created a young girl's nonprofit organization. Our vision started out as a mentorship program in the form of a talent directive company. We would host events every quarter showcasing the unique talents and gifts of young ladies whether ripping the runway (modeling), talent shows or High School Musical's. We want to be able to offer some guidance and give direction to girls who a lot of times remind me of myself growing up. I have been lost. I have struggled with self-esteem issues. But I have ultimately triumphed through it all! I aspire to be a resource within every community that one day I can share my curriculum and encouragement with.

I had an enormous amount of talent but little to no direction in my adolescent years. I desperately needed **positive** attention, however most of the recognition I received was unhealthy. 9 times out of 10 it came from members of the opposite sex that in turn would be completely harmful.

My goal is so much more than your typical talent agency!

We want to:
- Be an encouraging resource in the community

- Gain the trust of parents, care providers and ultimately young girls who aspire to be better than statistics show they will be.

- Implement our mentoring programs in schools around the world

- Guide and direct student with the mindset that their skills and talents should not go unnoticed.

- Empower young girls to step into their purpose and face their fears firsthand regardless of what anyone else says or does!

- And so much more!!

It's All About You Talent Sevices

501c3 organization

Made in the USA
Columbia, SC
04 May 2021